WINDOWS **11** MADE EASY, A HANDBOOK FOR SENIORS AND FIRST-TIME USERS

OVERCOME SETUP CHALLENGES, SIMPLIFY TASKS, AND PERSONALIZE YOUR EXPERIENCE WHILE EASING FEARS OF MISTAKES AND COMPLEX TERMINOLOGY

GARY MOSS

TABLE OF CONTENTS

INTRODUCTION

When Sylvia finally upgraded her computer, she was excited to explore the new features of Windows 11. But as soon as she turned it on, she felt overwhelmed. The familiar layout she knew from Windows 7 was replaced by strange icons and menus. Like many seniors and beginners, Sylvia wondered if she could get the hang of this new system.

If you've ever felt like Sylvia, this book is not just for you, it's about you. Your journey with Windows 11 is important to us. The goal here is to make Windows 11 approachable and easy to use. Whether you're new to computers or just new to this version of Windows, this book will guide you step-by-step. We'll tackle setup challenges, simplify tasks, and help you personalize your experience.

Why is this book important? Because in today's digital age, knowing how to use your computer is more than a skill—it's a necessity. From staying in touch with family and friends to managing your finances, many of your daily tasks can be done more easily with a computer. Windows 11 might seem daunting at first, but it opens up a world of possibilities once you get the hang of it.

This book is organized to make your learning process as smooth as possible. We start with the basics: turning on your computer and navigating the new Start menu. From there, we connect to the internet, set up email, and manage files. Each chapter focuses on a specific task, with clear instructions and plenty of pictures to guide you. At the end of each chapter, you'll find a summary and a quiz to help reinforce what you've learned. And if you run into any issues, there's a troubleshooting guide to help you.

I'm Gary Moss, and I love helping seniors and beginners overcome their tech-related challenges. Technology doesn't have to be intimidating. With the right guidance, anyone can learn to use it confidently. My passion for teaching and my experience in the field have driven me to write this book. I've seen firsthand how empowering it is for someone to finally feel comfortable using their computer.

What will you gain from reading this book? Confidence, for starters. By the time you finish, you'll be comfortable navigating Windows 11. You'll be able to easily perform everyday tasks and even explore some of the more advanced features. This book aims to remove the fear of making mistakes and to simplify the complex terminology that often comes with technology.

So, how do you get started? Just turn the page and follow along. Take your time with each chapter. Don't rush. The goal is to make sure you understand each step before moving on to the next. And remember, this book is not just a guide, it's your supportive tool. If you get stuck, refer to the troubleshooting guides or revisit the quizzes and summaries. We're here for you every step of the way.

In summary, this book is your companion in navigating Windows 11. It's designed to make the process straightforward and stress-free. By the end, you'll be proficient in using your computer and feel confident in exploring new features and tools.

Ready to tackle Windows 11? Let's get started! This book is not just a guide; it's an invitation to a new world of possibilities. It's time to unlock your computer's potential and start your journey with Windows 11.

1

GETTING STARTED WITH WINDOWS 11

When my friend John received his new laptop as a birthday gift, he was both excited and apprehensive. He had heard great things about Windows 11 but wasn't sure where to start. This chapter is designed specifically for those like John who are eager to explore their new device but need a little guidance to get started. Setting up a new computer can feel overwhelming, but with clear instructions and a bit of patience, you'll find it's quite manageable. We'll walk through each step, ensuring you understand the process and feel confident as you begin your journey with Windows 11.

1.1 UNBOXING AND SETTING UP YOUR NEW WINDOWS 11 DEVICE

First things first—unboxing your new device. A certain thrill comes with opening a brand-new gadget, but it's important to handle everything carefully to avoid any mishaps. As you unbox, make sure to check for all the necessary components. You should find the device itself, a power adapter, a user manual, and possibly some additional accessories like a mouse or a protective case. Take your time to remove each item gently from the packaging to avoid dropping anything.

Once you have everything out of the box, place your laptop or desktop on a stable surface. Avoid areas near the edge of tables or other precarious spots where it could easily fall. Before we dive into turning it on, let's ensure you have a safe setup. Keep drinks and other liquids away from your computer to prevent any accidental spills. Additionally, make sure your work area is free from clutter to avoid tripping over cables or knocking over your device.

Now, let's get your device powered up. Locate the power adapter and connect it to your computer. For laptops, you'll typically find the power port on the side, while desktops usually have it at the back. Plug the other end of the adapter into a wall outlet. It's a good idea to use a surge protector to guard against electrical surges that could damage your new device. Once connected, press the power button. On laptops, this button is often located above the keyboard or on the side. For desktops, it's usually on the front of the tower.

As your computer turns on, you'll see the Windows logo appear on the screen (shown to the left). This is a good sign—your device is booting up properly. The first screen you encounter will ask you to select your language and region settings. Take your time to choose the options that match your preferences. This step is crucial as it sets the default language for your system and ensures your region-specific settings, like time and date, are accurate.

Setting up a new device takes time, so patience is key. The initial setup process can take several minutes as the system configures itself and prepares for use. You might see a few screens with messages like "Just a moment" or "Getting things ready." It's important to let the process complete without interruptions. Use this time to familiarize yourself with the look and feel of your new computer, but avoid clicking or pressing buttons unnecessarily.

During the boot-up process, your screen will prompt you to select your keyboard layout. This might seem like a minor detail, but it ensures that all keys function as expected, especially if you use special characters or multiple languages. Once you've made your selections, the system will proceed to connect to your Wi-Fi network. Make sure you have your Wi-Fi password handy, as you'll need it to complete this step.

Finally, you'll be greeted with the Windows 11 welcome screen. This marks the end of the initial setup and the beginning of your exploration of this new operating system. Remember, the key to a smooth setup is taking it one step at a time. Don't rush through the screens, and if you're ever unsure, refer back to this guide. With each step, you're closer to mastering the essentials of your new Windows 11 device.

1.2 COMPLETING THE INITIAL WINDOWS 11 SETUP

Once your device is powered on, you'll be greeted by the Windows 11 setup wizard. This is where you'll make the initial selections that tailor your computer to your preferences. The first screen will prompt you to choose your language, time, and keyboard preferences. This step ensures that your device communicates with you in a way that feels natural and familiar. Select your preferred language from the dropdown menu, then confirm your time zone and keyboard layout. It's essential to get these settings right as they influence the overall user experience. Take a moment to double-check your selections before moving on.

Next, you'll connect to a Wi-Fi network. This step is crucial as it enables your device to access the internet, download updates, and complete the setup process. A list of available networks will appear on your screen. Select your network and enter the password if prompted. If you're unsure of your Wi-Fi password, you can usually find it on the back of your router. Once connected, your device may perform a quick check to ensure the connection is stable. This step might take a few moments, so be patient and let the system do its work.

The setup wizard will then guide you through creating or signing in with a Microsoft account. This account allows you to access various Microsoft services, such as OneDrive, Office, and the Microsoft Store. If you already have an account, enter your email address and password. If not, follow the prompts to create a new one. This process includes verifying your email address and setting up security questions to help recover your account if you forget your password. A Microsoft account is beneficial for syncing settings and files across multiple devices, like your phone or tablet for instance. making your experience more seamless.

Privacy settings are an integral part of your initial setup, and it's crucial to understand what you're agreeing to. The wizard will present several privacy options, including location services, diagnostic data sharing, and ad personalization. Location services allow apps to determine your location for better accuracy in maps and weather apps. If you value privacy over convenience, you may choose to disable this feature. Diagnostic data sharing helps Microsoft improve their services by sending usage data back to them. You can opt for basic data sharing or turn it off entirely. Ad personalization tailors advertisements to your interests based on your browsing history. If you prefer not to have personalized ads, you can also disable this feature. Take your time to read through each option and select what feels right for you.These initial steps are important, so please take your time.

Security is another critical aspect of setting up your new device. The wizard will prompt you to create a strong password. A secure password combines letters, numbers, and special characters, making it hard to guess. Avoid using common words or easily accessible information like birthdays. Once your password is set, consider enabling two-factor authentication (2F. This adds an extra layer of security by requiring a second piece of information, such as a code sent to your phone, to log in. Enabling 2FA significantly reduces the risk of unauthorized access to your account, providing peace of mind. I use these on all of my accounts.

Finally, let's talk about updates. Allowing Windows to check for and install updates during the setup process is vital for both security and functionality. Updates often include patches for security vulnerabilities, new features, and improvements to existing ones. To ensure your system remains stable and secure, make sure automatic updates are enabled. The setup wizard will guide you through this process, checking for any available updates and installing them as needed. This step might take some time, but it's worth the wait to have the latest protections and features right from the start.

Throughout this setup process, remember that each step is designed to customize your device to suit your needs best. Take your time, read each prompt carefully, and make selections that align with your preferences. The setup wizard is your guide, designed to make this process straightforward and stress-free.

1.3 UNDERSTANDING THE WINDOWS 11 DESKTOP LAYOUT

When you first see the Windows 11 desktop, it might look a bit different from what you're used to. Let's break it down so you can feel comfortable and confident navigating it. The desktop is your main workspace, where you'll find the Start menu, taskbar, and system tray. The Start menu is the Windows icon all the way to the left of the example. Clicking this button opens a menu that gives you access to your apps, settings, and files. It's designed to be your main hub for finding everything you need.

The taskbar itself is a strip at the bottom of your screen that holds icons for your most-used apps, currently open applications, and system notifications. You'll see small icons representing different programs, and clicking on any of these will open the respective application. On the far right of the taskbar, you'll find the system tray, which contains icons for background apps and system functions like network status, battery level, and sound settings. These icons give you quick access to essential functions and notifications. In the example above, it is all the way to the right. Left of the time and date. To access it, click the wifi and speaker icon.

Desktop icons are another key element you'll encounter. These small images represent various programs and files on your computer. For example, there's the File Explorer icon, which looks like a little yellow folder (also shown in the example above). File Explorer helps you navigate through your files and folders, making it easy to find documents, photos, and other data. Lastly, you'll likely see the Microsoft Edge icon, which resembles a wave. This is your web browser, used for accessing the internet. You can find these by hovering over the icons in your taskbar with your pointer.

Understanding Windows and open applications is crucial for multitasking. Each open application appears in its own window. The title bar at the top of each window displays the name of the application or document. On the right side of the title bar, you'll find three control buttons: minimize, maximize, and close. The minimize button, represented by a dash, hides the window without closing it. You can bring it back by clicking its icon in the taskbar. The maximize button, symbolized by a square, enlarges the window to fill the entire screen. Clicking it again will restore the window to its previous size. The close button, marked by an "X," will close the window entirely. Below is an example. You can see the three control buttons all the way to the right.

Taskbar previews are a handy feature to manage your open windows. Hovering your mouse over an application icon in the taskbar shows a small preview of that window. This allows you to quickly see what's happening in each open application without switching between them. It's particularly useful if you have multiple documents or web pages open and need to find the right one quickly.

Using visual aids can greatly enhance your understanding of the desktop layout. As you read through this section, refer to the screenshots and annotations provided. These images will give you a visual representation of what each element looks like, making it easier to follow along. For instance, you might see a screenshot of the taskbar with labels pointing to the Start menu, taskbar icons, and system tray. This visual context helps solidify your comprehension of the workspace.

Imagine setting up your desk at home, where each item has a specific place. Your computer monitor and keyboard are in the center, similar to how the Start menu is centrally located. The taskbar icons are like the tools and supplies you keep within arm's reach for easy access. The system tray resembles a drawer containing essential items, always available but neatly tucked away.

Now that you have a clearer understanding of the Windows 11 desktop layout, you can navigate your new device with confidence. Each element is designed to help you work efficiently and access your applications and files with ease.

1.4 NAVIGATING THE START MENU AND TASKBAR

Understanding the Start menu is crucial for navigating Windows 11 effectively. This central hub is where you'll access your apps, settings, and files.You can access it by clicking the Windows icon (the blue 4 squares) in the taskbar. The Start menu is divided into several sections, each with a specific function. At the top, you'll find pinned apps and tiles. These are shortcuts to your most frequently used applications, allowing you to open them quickly without searching. You can pin any app here by right-clicking it and selecting "Pin to Start." This section is customizable, letting you arrange and resize tiles to fit your preferences. Below or to the right the pinned apps, you'll see the "All Apps" list. Clicking on this option opens a comprehensive list of all the applications installed on your device, organized alphabetically. This is particularly useful when you need to find an app that isn't pinned to the Start menu.In the bottom right corner is where you find your power options. You can power on, off or restart your computer. Finally, at the bottom left, you'll find user profile and account options. Here, you can switch accounts, sign out, or access your account settings. This area ensures you can manage your user preferences and settings easily. Here is an example of the start menu.

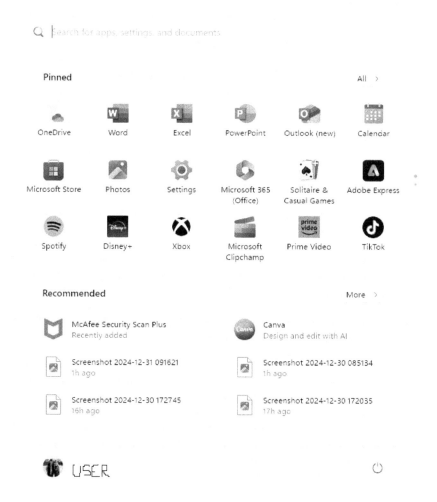

Customizing the Start menu to suit your needs can greatly enhance your Windows 11 experience. To pin an app to the Start menu, simply right-click on the app icon and select "Pin to Start." This adds the app to your pinned section, making it accessible with a single click. If you want to remove an app, right-click on the tile and select "Unpin from Start." You can also rearrange the tiles by clicking and dragging them to your desired position. Resizing tiles is another way to personalize your Start menu. Right-click on a tile, hover over "Resize," and choose from the available size options. This allows you to fit more apps on your Start menu or highlight the ones you use most often. Adding new shortcuts is straightforward as well. Simply find the app in the "All Apps" list, right-click on it, and select "Pin to Start." This customization makes it easier to access your favorite apps quickly and efficiently.

The taskbar is another essential part of your Windows 11 interface. It sits at the bottom of your screen and provides quick access to your apps, system notifications, and the Start menu. Pinning apps to the taskbar is similar to pinning them to the Start menu. Right-click on an app and select "Pin to taskbar." This places the app icon on the taskbar, allowing you to open it with a single click. If you want to remove an app from the taskbar, right-click on the icon and select "Unpin from the taskbar." The search bar on the taskbar is a powerful tool for finding files, apps, and settings quickly. Simply click on the search bar and start typing what you're looking for. Windows will display a list of relevant results, making it easy to find what you need without navigating through menus. Managing system notifications is also straightforward. Click on the notification icon on the far right of the taskbar to open the Action Center. Here, you'll see notifications from various apps and system alerts. You can dismiss notifications by clicking the "X" next to each one or clear all notifications at once. Below is another example of the taskbar.

Customizing the taskbar's appearance and behavior can make your Windows 11 experience more enjoyable and efficient. To change the taskbar's alignment, right-click on the taskbar and select "Taskbar settings." Scroll down to "Taskbar behaviors" and choose between centering the Start button or aligning it to the left. You can also adjust the taskbar color and transparency through the settings menu. Go to Settings > Personalization > Colors, and choose your preferred color and transparency settings. This allows you to personalize the look of your taskbar to match your style and preferences. Additionally, you can enable or disable taskbar features like showing badges on taskbar buttons or hiding the taskbar automatically when not in use. These settings help you create a clean and functional workspace tailored to your needs.

1.5 USING BASIC MOUSE AND KEYBOARD FUNCTIONS

Understanding how to use your mouse and keyboard effectively will make your experience with Windows 11 much smoother. Let's start with the basic mouse functions. The left-click is your primary action button. Use it to select items, open links, and interact with most elements on your screen. For example, left-clicking on an icon will select it, while left-clicking on a button in a program will activate it. The right-click, on the other hand, opens context menus. These menus provide additional options related to the item you clicked on. For instance, right-clicking on a file icon might give you options to rename, delete, or view properties. Below is a example of what you might see when you right click.

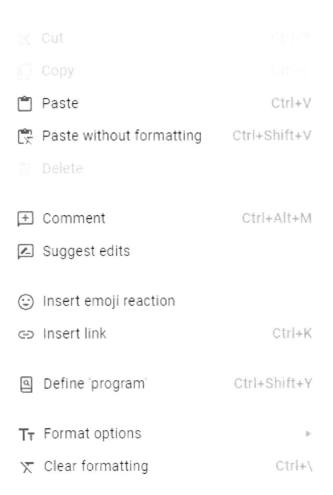

The double-click action is used to open files and folders. For example, double-clicking on a folder in File Explorer will open it, allowing you to view its contents. This action is performed by quickly pressing the left mouse button twice. Practice this a few times to get the hang of it. Another useful mouse function is drag-and-drop. This allows you to move files or folders from one location to another. Click and hold the left mouse button on the item you want to move. Then, drag it to the desired location and release the mouse button. This function is handy for organizing your files.

Now, let's talk about keyboard shortcuts. These combinations of keys can save you a lot of time and make your workflow more efficient. One of the most common shortcuts is Copy (Ctrl + and Paste (Ctrl + V). Use these to duplicate text or files from one place to another. For example, if you have written a sentence that you want to use in another document, highlight the text, press Ctrl + C to copy it, navigate to the new document, and press Ctrl + V to paste it. The Undo (Ctrl + Z) and Redo (Ctrl + Y) shortcuts are equally useful. If you make a mistake, press Ctrl + Z to undo the last action. If you change your mind, press Ctrl + Y to redo it.

Switching between open applications is another area where keyboard shortcuts shine. Pressing Alt + Tab allows you to cycle through all the open programs on your computer. Hold down the Alt key, then press Tab to switch to the next open application. Release both keys to bring the selected application to the forefront. This is particularly useful if you are working on multiple tasks simultaneously and need to switch back and forth quickly.

For those using a laptop, the touchpad can serve as an alternative to the mouse. Basic touchpad gestures mimic mouse actions. A single tap on the touchpad is equivalent to a left-click, allowing you to select items. A two-finger tap acts as a right-click, opening context menus. You can also use two fingers to scroll up and down, similar to using the scroll wheel on a mouse. Mastering these gestures can make navigating your laptop much more efficient.

Accessibility options are available to make mouse and keyboard usage easier, especially for those with physical limitations. Adjusting the mouse pointer size and speed can make it easier to see and control. Go to Settings > Devices > Mouse, where you can customize these settings to suit your needs. For keyboard settings, explore options like Sticky Keys and Filter Keys. Sticky Keys allow you to press one key at a time for keyboard shortcuts instead of holding them down simultaneously. Filter Keys help prevent accidental repeated keystrokes by ignoring brief or repeated presses.

In conclusion, understanding these basic mouse and keyboard functions will greatly enhance your interaction with Windows 11. Whether you are selecting items, navigating through applications, or customizing settings for accessibility, mastering these functions will make your computing experience more efficient and enjoyable. Remember, practice makes perfect. Spend some time getting comfortable with these functions, and soon they will become second nature.

QUIZ: CHAPTER 1 - GETTING STARTED WITH WINDOWS 11

Questions

1. **What should you do first when unboxing your new Windows 11 device?**

   a. Turn on the computer immediately
   b. Handle items carefully and check for all necessary components
   c. Connect to the internet
   d. Skip reading the user manual

2. **Why is it recommended to use a surge protector when setting up your new device?**

   a. To improve the battery life of your device
   b. To avoid accidental power outages
   c. To protect your device from electrical surges

d. To ensure faster charging

3. **What is the purpose of selecting your language and region during the initial setup?**

a. To enhance the speed of your device
b. To set default system preferences, such as language and time zone
c. To register your device with Microsoft
d. To prevent unauthorized access to your device

4. **Which of the following is NOT part of the Windows 11 desktop layout?**

a. Start menu
b. Taskbar
c. System tray
d. File Explorer menu bar

5. **What is the function of the Alt + Tab keyboard shortcut in Windows 11?**

a. To close an application
b. To copy and paste text
c. To switch between open applications
d. To open the task manager

2

CONNECTING TO THE INTERNET

I magine you've just finished setting up your new Windows 11 computer, and now you're eager to explore everything it has to offer. The next crucial step is connecting your device to the internet. An internet connection is essential if you want to browse the web, check emails, or stream your favorite shows. In this chapter, we'll guide you through setting up both Wi-Fi and Ethernet connections, ensuring you understand the benefits and limitations of each.

2.1 CONNECTING TO THE INTERNET

When it comes to connecting to the internet, you have two main options: Wi-Fi and Ethernet. Wi-Fi offers the convenience of wireless connectivity (no cables to plug in), allowing you to use your computer anywhere within the range of your router. This is particularly useful if you like moving around your home with your laptop or if your computer is far from the router. However, Wi-Fi can sometimes be less stable, especially in areas with many electronic devices or thick walls that interfere with the signal. On the other hand, Ethernet provides a stable and faster connection because it uses a physical cable to connect your computer directly to the router. This makes it an excellent choice for tasks that require a lot of bandwidth, like streaming high-definition videos or online gaming. The downside is that it limits your mobility, as you need to stay close to the router.

To set up a Wi-Fi connection, start by accessing the network settings on your Windows 11 device. Click on the Network, Sound, or Battery icons on the far right side of the taskbar to open the quick settings menu (the wifi signal and speaker icons). From there, select "Manage Wi-Fi connections." A list of available Wi-Fi networks will appear. Choose your network from the list and click "Connect." The network you choose should be your network, so you can make sure it is secure. You'll be prompted to enter the network password, which is usually found on a sticker on your router or provided by your internet service provider. After typing in the password, click "Next." Your computer will then attempt to connect to the network. If everything is set up correctly, you should see a message indicating a successful connection. If you encounter issues, such as the network not appearing in the list or a failed connection attempt, try restarting your router or moving closer to it. Sometimes, simply turning your Wi-Fi off and on again can resolve minor connectivity problems.

Setting up an Ethernet connection is straightforward. First, locate the Ethernet port on your device. On a laptop, this port is usually found on the side, while on a desktop, it's typically located at the back of the tower. Take an Ethernet cable and connect one end to your computer's Ethernet port and the other end to an available port on your router. Once connected, your device should automatically detect the Ethernet connection and connect to the internet. To verify the connection, click on the Network icon in the taskbar. You should see an indication that you are connected via Ethernet.

This method provides a reliable and fast internet connection, making it ideal for activities that demand consistent high-speed internet.

To optimize your internet connection, whether you're using Wi-Fi or Ethernet, there are a few tips to keep in mind. For Wi-Fi users, the position of your router plays a significant role in the strength and stability of your connection. Place the router in a central location, elevated from the ground and away from obstructions like walls and large metal objects. This helps to ensure a strong signal throughout your home. Additionally, using a quality Ethernet cable can make a big difference if you opt for a wired connection. Look for cables that are rated for higher speeds, such as Cat6 or Cat7, which provide better performance and reliability.

Regularly checking for firmware updates on your router can also improve your internet connection. Manufacturers often release updates to fix bugs, enhance performance, and provide additional features. To update your router's firmware, log in to the router's web interface. The address is usually printed on the router itself. Look for the firmware or update section and follow the manufacturer's instructions. Keeping your router's firmware up-to-date ensures you get the best possible performance and security.

Connecting to the internet opens up a world of possibilities with your new Windows 11 device. By understanding the differences between Wi-Fi and Ethernet and following the setup steps, you can ensure a smooth and enjoyable online experience.

2.2 BROWSING THE WEB WITH MICROSOFT EDGE

Microsoft Edge

Now that you're connected to the internet, the next step is to familiarize yourself with browsing using Microsoft Edge. This web browser is designed to be user-friendly and efficient, making it ideal for beginners and experienced users. To get started, open Microsoft Edge by clicking on its icon, which looks like a blue wave(shown above), located either on your desktop or in the taskbar. When you first open Edge, you'll be greeted by a clean, organized interface. At the top, you'll find the address bar, which is your gateway to the entire internet. This is where you'll type web addresses or search terms. Edge will either take you directly to the website you entered or show you search results related to your query. To the left of the address bar, you'll see the back, forward, and refresh buttons. Here is what they look like.

These tools help you navigate through web pages. The back button takes you to the previous page, the forward button moves you to the next page if you've gone back, and the refresh button reloads the current page. On the right side of the address bar, you'll find a star icon for adding favorites, a three-dot menu for more options, and your profile icon. Here is what they look like.

Browsing the web is a straightforward process with Microsoft Edge. To visit a website, click on the address bar, type in the URL (such as www.example.com), and press Enter. Edge will load the website and display it in the main window. If you're not sure of the exact address, you can type keywords or questions directly into the address bar, and Edge will show search results from your default search engine. Once you're on a web page, you'll often see blue, underlined text known as hyperlinks. Clicking on these links takes you to another page within the same website or to a different site altogether. This is a common way to navigate the web and find related information. If you want to go back to the previous page, simply click the back button(the left arrow on the left of the search bar). Conversely, if you've gone back and want to return to the page you were on, click the forward button(the right arrow to the left of the search bar). If a page isn't loading correctly or you want to see the latest content, use the refresh button(te circle with the arrow to the left of the search bar).

Customizing your browser settings can enhance your browsing experience. To access these settings, click on the three-dot menu in the upper right corner and select "Settings." (An example of that menu is below.) Under the "Appearance" section, you can change the theme of Edge, adjust the size of the text, and choose which buttons appear on the toolbar. You can also set your home page, which is the first page you see when you open Edge. To do this, go to the "Start, home, and new tabs" section and enter the URL of your preferred home page. Additionally, you can change your default search engine. This is the engine that Edge uses when you type a query into the address bar. To change it, go to "Privacy, search, and services," scroll down to "Services," and click "Address bar and search." From there, you can select a different search engine from the dropdown menu.

Browser extensions are tools that add extra functionality to your browsing experience. Think of them as small apps you can install within Edge to make certain tasks easier. To explore available extensions, click on the three-dot menu, select "Extensions," and then click "Open Microsoft Edge Add-ons store." Here, you'll find a wide range of extensions, from ad blockers that remove advertisements from web pages to password managers that securely store your login credentials. To install an extension, find one that interests you, click "Get," and follow the prompts. Once installed, the extension's icon will appear next to the address bar. To manage your extensions, go back to the Extensions menu. From here, you can enable or disable extensions, adjust their settings, or remove them entirely by clicking "Remove."

Navigating the web with Microsoft Edge becomes second nature with a bit of practice. The browser is designed to help you find information quickly and customize your experience to suit your needs. Whether you're looking up recipes, reading news articles, or shopping online, Edge provides a reliable and efficient way to browse the internet.

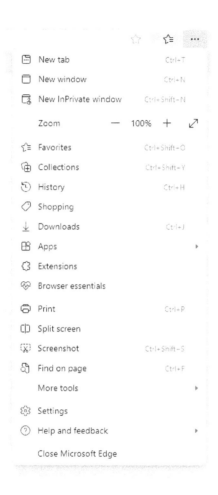

2.3 SAFE BROWSING PRACTICES

When you venture online, practicing safe browsing habits is crucial to protect your personal information. The internet is a vast resource, but it also harbors risks like malware and phishing attempts. Malware, short for malicious software, includes viruses and spyware that can damage your computer or steal your information. Phishing attacks involve deceptive emails or websites that trick you into revealing sensitive data like passwords or credit card numbers. By adopting safe browsing habits, you minimize these risks and make your online experience more secure and enjoyable.

Recognizing secure websites is one of the first steps in safe browsing. A secure website uses HTTPS in its URL, which stands for HyperText Transfer Protocol Secure. This means the data exchanged between your browser and the website is encrypted, making it harder for attackers to intercept. Always look for HTTPS at the beginning of a web address before entering any personal information. Additionally, secure sites often display a padlock icon next to the URL. Clicking on this padlock provides more details about the website's security certificate. Avoid sites that trigger suspicious pop-ups or ask for personal information without displaying these security signs. These pop-ups can be a sign of malicious intent, leading you to unsafe websites or downloads.

Microsoft Edge includes several built-in security features to enhance your browsing safety. One such feature is the SmartScreen filter, which helps protect you from phishing and malware attacks by blocking potentially dangerous websites and downloads. To enable SmartScreen, click on the three-dot menu in the upper right corner, go to "Settings," then "Privacy, search, and services." Scroll down to "Security" and ensure the SmartScreen filter is turned on. Another useful feature is the InPrivate browsing mode. This mode prevents Edge from saving your browsing history, cookies, and temporary files. To start an InPrivate session, click on the three-dot menu and select "New InPrivate window." This is particularly handy when using a shared computer or if you want to keep your browsing activities private.

Creating strong passwords is another critical component of online security. A strong password typically includes a mix of letters, numbers, and special characters, making it difficult to guess. Avoid common passwords like "123456" or "password," which are easy targets for hackers. Instead, use a combination of unrelated words, numbers, and symbols. For example, "Blu3$kY!29" is much harder to crack than "John123." Managing multiple strong passwords can be challenging, which is where a password manager comes in handy. Password managers store and encrypt your passwords, allowing you to access them easily and securely. Microsoft Edge has a built-in password manager that you can enable by going to "Settings," then "Profiles," and selecting "Passwords." Here, you can save and auto-fill passwords for various websites, reducing the need to remember each one individually.

Avoiding common password mistakes is equally important. Never use the same password across multiple sites. If one account gets compromised, all your other accounts with the same password are at risk. Also, steer clear of using easily accessible information, such as your name or birthdate, in your passwords. Hackers can often find this information through social media or public records. Regularly updating your passwords and using two-factor authentication (2F adds an extra layer of security. 2FA requires a second form of verification, such as a code sent to your phone, in addition to your password. Many websites and services offer 2FA, and I highly recommended to enable it wherever possible.

By adhering to these practices, you can significantly reduce the risks associated with browsing the internet. Safe browsing protects your personal information and ensures a smoother, more enjoyable online experience.

2.4 MANAGING BROWSER TABS AND BOOKMARKS

One of the most useful features of Microsoft Edge is the ability to open and manage multiple tabs. Tabs allow you to have several web pages open simultaneously, making it easier to switch between different websites without losing your place. To open a new tab, simply click on the small plus sign (+) next to your current tab at the top of the browser window. A new blank tab will appear, ready for you to enter a web address or perform a search. Switching between tabs is as simple as clicking on the tab you want to view. Each tab displays the title of the web page, making it easy to identify. If you need to close a tab, click on the small "X" on the tab itself. Managing multiple tabs efficiently can significantly enhance your browsing experience, allowing you to keep important pages readily accessible.

Organizing your tabs into groups can further streamline your browsing. Tab groups allow you to categorize your tabs, making it easier to manage related web pages. To create a new tab group, right-click on a tab and select "Add to new group." You can then name the group and choose a color to help distinguish it. Adding tabs to a group is as simple as right-clicking on a tab and selecting "Add to existing group," then choosing the desired group. This feature is particularly useful if you're working on a project that requires multiple resources or if you want to keep your personal and work-related tabs separate. Removing a tab from a group is just as easy—right-click on the tab and select "Remove from group." Naming and color-coding your tab groups can make your browsing experience more organized and visually appealing.

Bookmarks, also known as favorites, are another powerful tool for managing your favorite websites. To add a bookmark, navigate to the web page you want to save and click on the star icon in the address bar. A dialog box will appear, allowing you to name the bookmark and choose where to save it. The bookmarks bar is a convenient place to keep your most frequently visited sites. To enable the bookmarks bar, click on the three-dot menu, go to "Settings," then "Appearance," and toggle the switch for "Show favorites bar." You can also organize your bookmarks into folders for better management. Right-click on the bookmarks bar and select "Add folder." Name the folder and drag and drop bookmarks into it. Editing your bookmarks is straightforward—right-click on a bookmark and select "Edit," where you can rename or change the URL. This organization makes it easy to quickly access your favorite sites without having to search for them every time.

The Reading List feature in Microsoft Edge is perfect for saving articles and web pages to read later. If you come across an interesting article but don't have time to read it immediately, you can add it to your Reading List for future reference. To add an item to the Reading List, click on the star icon in the address bar, then select "Reading List" from the options. Click "Add" to save the page. To access your Reading List, click on the three-line menu (also known as the hu in the upper right corner, then select "Reading List." Here, you'll see all the saved pages organized by date. You can click on any item to open it, or right-click to remove it from the list once you've read it. This feature ensures that you never miss out on interesting content and can catch up at your convenience.

Managing browser tabs and bookmarks efficiently can transform how you navigate the web, making your online activities more organized and accessible. These features are designed to enhance your browsing experience by allowing you to keep track of multiple sites and save valuable content for later. By mastering these tools, you can make the most out of your time spent online, ensuring a smooth and enjoyable browsing experience.

2.5 DOWNLOADING AND MANAGING FILES FROM THE INTERNET

Downloading files from the internet can be incredibly useful, whether you're saving documents, images, or software. However, it's essential to download files safely to avoid potential risks such as malware or unwanted programs. Recognizing safe download sources is the first step. Stick to reputable websites and official sources. For example, if you need a software update or a new application, visit the official website of the software provider. Avoid clicking on download links from unknown emails or suspicious websites. These can often lead to malicious files that might harm your computer or compromise your personal information. If you're unsure, look for reviews or ratings of the download source.

When you're ready to download a file using Microsoft Edge, the process is straightforward. Begin by clicking on the download link of the file you wish to obtain (this will be a square box with an arrow pointing down inside or an arrow pointing down to a line). Edge will prompt you with a dialog box asking whether you want to run or save the file. It's generally safer to save the file first so you can scan it for any potential threats before opening it. Once you click "Save," Edge will start downloading the file. You can monitor the progress at the bottom of the browser window. The download bar will show the file name, size, and the percentage completed. If you need to pause or cancel the download, options are available directly within this bar. Once the download is complete, you can click on the file name to open it or go to your designated download folder to locate it.

Keeping your downloaded files organized is crucial for easy access. By default, downloaded files are saved in the "Downloads" folder. You can set a different default download location by clicking on the three-dot menu in Edge, selecting "Settings," then

"Downloads," and choosing your preferred folder. After down-loading, it's a good habit to move files to specific folders based on their type or purpose. For instance, create separate folders for documents, photos, and software. This organization helps you find files quickly without sifting through a cluttered downloads folder. To move a file, right-click on it, select "Cut," navigate to the desired folder, and then right-click and select "Paste."

Compressed files, like ZIP files, are common when downloading multiple files or large applications. These files need to be extracted before you can use their contents. To handle ZIP files and other compressed formats, you'll need a file extraction tool. A popular choice is 7-Zip, which is free and easy to use. Download and install 7-Zip from its official website. Once installed, navigate to the ZIP file you downloaded, right-click on it, and select "7-Zip" followed by "Extract Here" or "Extract to [folder name]." This action will unpack the contents of the ZIP file into the specified location, making the files accessible for use.

Handling downloads and managing files efficiently ensures you can make the most out of your internet browsing experience. By following these steps, you can safely download, organize, and utilize files from the internet, keeping your digital workspace tidy and secure.

By now, you should feel more confident in connecting to the internet and managing your online activities. From setting up Wi-Fi and Ethernet connections to browsing safely and downloading files securely, you've learned essential skills that make your Windows 11 experience smoother and more enjoyable.

QUIZ: CHAPTER 2 - CONNECTING TO THE INTERNET

Questions

1. **What is one primary advantage of using Ethernet over Wi-Fi?**

   a. It allows you to move your computer anywhere in the house.
   b. It provides a stable and faster connection.
   c. It eliminates the need for a router.
   d. It does not require any cables.

2. **Where can you find your Wi-Fi password if you don't remember it?**

   a. In the Windows 11 settings menu.
   b. Printed on your router or provided by your internet service provider.
   c. On the back of your laptop.
   d. In the Microsoft Edge browser settings.

3. **What feature of Microsoft Edge protects you from phishing and malware?**

   a. Address bar shortcuts.
   b. SmartScreen filter.
   c. Browser themes.
   d. Tab grouping.

4. **How can you save a website to access it later in Microsoft Edge?**

a. Click the star icon in the address bar to add it to bookmarks or favorites.
b. Use the browser's search bar to type the name of the website.
c. Right-click the browser tab and select "Save Page."
d. Open the website in a new tab and leave it open.

5. **What is a key characteristic of a strong password?**

a. It uses only letters and numbers.
b. It is short and easy to remember.
c. It includes a mix of letters, numbers, and special characters.
d. It matches your username for easy recall.

3

PERSONALIZING YOUR WINDOWS 11 EXPERIENCE

I magine being able to transform your computer screen into a reflection of your unique style and preferences. Personalizing your Windows 11 experience is not only about aesthetics; it's about making your digital space feel comfortable and familiar. This chapter will guide you through various ways to customize your desktop, ensuring it resonates with your personal taste and needs.

3.1 CHANGING DESKTOP BACKGROUNDS AND THEMES

Changing your desktop background is one of the simplest ways to personalize your computer. A new wallpaper can instantly refresh your workspace, making it feel more inviting. To begin, click on the Start menu (the four blue squares) and select Settings. From here, navigate to Personalization and then click on Background. You'll see several options: you can choose from the pre-installed images, select a solid color, or upload your own photos. If you opt to use your own images, click on the 'Browse' button, find the picture you want from the pictures or files you have put in your computer, and select it. Watching your favorite photo appear on your desktop can bring a touch of joy every time you turn on your computer.

Themes offer a deeper level of customization by changing multiple elements of your desktop at once. Themes can modify colors, sounds, and even mouse cursors, providing a cohesive look. To access themes, go to Settings, then Personalization, and click on Themes. Here, you can choose from various pre-installed themes or download new ones from the Microsoft Store. Once you select a theme, it will apply changes across your desktop, giving it a new look and feel. You can further customize these themes by altering individual components. For example, you can change the theme colors to match your favorite shades, adjust the system sounds to something more pleasant, or even choose a fun cursor design. This way, your computer becomes an extension of yourself, tailored to your preferences.

For those who enjoy variety, setting up a slideshow background can be an exciting way to keep your desktop fresh. A slideshow allows you to select multiple images that rotate at intervals you choose. To set this up, go to Settings, then Personalization, and select Background. Choose Slideshow from the dropdown menu. Click on Browse to select the folder containing your chosen images. You can then set the interval time between image changes, ranging from every minute to once a day. This feature keeps your desktop dynamic, showcasing a new image at regular intervals and ensuring you never get bored with your background.

Finding high-quality wallpapers and themes online can further enhance your desktop's appearance. Websites like Unsplash and Pexels offer numerous stunning images you can download for free. The Microsoft Store is a safe and convenient place to explore various options for themes. Always ensure that you download images and themes from trusted sources to avoid any potential risks. Once downloaded, adding them to your desktop is straightforward—simply follow the steps outlined above to upload your new images or apply your new themes.

By customizing your desktop background and themes, you create a digital environment that feels uniquely yours. These simple changes can make a significant difference in how you interact with your computer, making it more enjoyable and personalized.

3.2 CUSTOMIZING THE TASKBAR AND START MENU

The taskbar (at the bottom of your screen) is a vital part of your Windows 11 experience, providing quick access to your favorite apps and important system functions. If you prefer your taskbar on a different edge of the screen, you can easily move it. Start by right-clicking on an empty area of the taskbar and selecting "Taskbar settings." Scroll down to "Taskbar behaviors" and find the "Taskbar alignment" option. Here, you can choose to align the taskbar to the left, right, top, or bottom of your screen. For a cleaner look, you might also want to enable the auto-hide feature. This setting hides the taskbar when it's not in use, giving you more screen space. To enable this, go to the same "Taskbar settings" menu and toggle on "Automatically hide the taskbar."

Pinning apps to the taskbar can save you time, allowing quick access to your most-used applications. To pin an app, find its icon either on the desktop or in the Start menu, right-click on it, and select "Pin to taskbar." This action places the app icon on the taskbar, making it accessible with a single click. If your taskbar starts to look cluttered, you can rearrange the icons. Click and drag an icon to a new position on the taskbar to organize them according to your preferences. This way, you can keep frequently used apps within easy reach and less-used apps further away.

Customizing the Start menu layout allows you to organize your apps and make your Start menu functional and visually appealing. To add a tile to the Start menu, find the app you want to add, right-click on it, and select "Pin to Start." This action places the app in the pinned section of the Start menu. If you want to remove a tile, right-click on it and select "Unpin from Start." You can also resize these tiles to fit your layout better. Right-click on a tile, hover over "Resize," and choose from the available size options. Organizing your tiles into groups can make your Start menu more intuitive. Drag and drop tiles into a new position to create a group, and then click above the group to name it. This organization helps you quickly find the apps you need.

Changing the color and transparency settings of the taskbar and Start menu can make your Windows 11 experience more personalized and visually pleasing. To change these settings, go to Settings, then Personalization, and click on Colors. Here, you can select an accent color that will be applied to the Start menu, taskbar, and other elements. If you prefer a subtler look, you can enable transparency effects. This setting gives the taskbar and Start menu a slightly see-through appearance, which can make your desktop look more modern and less cluttered. Toggle the "Transparency effects" option to turn this feature on or off. You can also choose between light and dark modes to match your preference. This customization makes your desktop not only functional but also aesthetically pleasing, reflecting your personal style.

By taking the time to customize the taskbar and Start menu, you make your daily interactions with Windows 11 more efficient and enjoyable. These adjustments can save you time and make your computer feel like an extension of your personal space. Whether you prefer a minimalist look or a vibrant, organized setup, these customization options allow you to tailor your desktop to your liking.

3.3 ADJUSTING DISPLAY SETTINGS FOR BETTER VISIBILITY

Customizing your display settings can make a significant differ-ence in how comfortable your computing experience is, especially if you spend a lot of time on your computer. To start, adjusting your screen resolution ensures that text and images appear sharp and clear. High resolution means better clarity, but it also makes items appear smaller. To change the screen resolution, click on the Start menu (the 4 blue squares) and select Settings. From there, navigate to System and then Display. You'll see a section called Display resolution. Click on the dropdown menu and choose the resolution that suits you best. If you're unsure, Windows usually recommends an optimal setting. Additionally, you can change the screen orientation from landscape to portrait. This is particularly useful if you read a lot of documents or e-books. Still within the Display settings, locate the Orientation dropdown menu and select either Landscape or Portrait. This adjustment rotates your screen to fit your needs.

For those who find text and other items too small, scaling and layout options can be a game-changer. Scaling adjusts the size of text, apps, and other elements to make them more readable. To access scaling settings, go to Settings, System, and then Display. In the Scale and layout section, you'll see a dropdown menu under Change the size of text, apps, and other items. Here, you can choose a percentage to increase the size of these elements. Windows offers standard scaling options like 100%, 125%, and 150%. If you need a custom size, click on Advanced scaling settings and enter the percentage you prefer. This feature ensures that everything on your screen is comfortably visible, reducing strain on your eyes.

Night light and color filters are invaluable for reducing eye strain, especially during extended use. Night light reduces the amount of blue light emitted by your screen, which can help you sleep better if you use your computer late at night. To enable Night light, go to Settings, System, and then Display. Under the Color section, you'll find the Night light toggle. Turn it on and click on Night light settings to customize it further. You can set a schedule for Night light to turn on and off automatically, usually from sunset to sunrise. Adjust the strength using the slider to find a comfortable level. For additional comfort, color filters can enhance visibility for users with color blindness or light sensitivity. In the same Display settings, find the Color filters section and toggle it on. Choose from various filters like grayscale or inverted colors to find the one that works best for you.

Adjusting the font size can also make a big difference in readability. Windows 11 allows you to increase or decrease the default font size across the system. To change the font size, go to Settings and then Accessibility. Select Text size, where you'll find a slider to adjust the font size. Move the slider to the right to increase the size or to the left to decrease it. You'll see a preview of the text size as you adjust the slider, so you can find the perfect setting before applying it. Once you're satisfied, click Apply. This change makes all text on your computer larger or smaller, depending on your preference, and is particularly useful for those with vision impairments.

Making these adjustments can significantly improve your comfort and productivity while using your computer. Whether you need to change the screen resolution, adjust scaling, enable night light, or increase font size, these settings are designed to make your Windows 11 experience as pleasant as possible. Navigating through the settings might seem daunting at first, but with a little patience, you'll find that these customizations are straightforward and immensely beneficial for better visibility and overall usability. You can explore it just by hitting the start button, going to settings, and checking out the options. It's a great way to learn about your settings.

3.4 SETTING UP USER ACCOUNTS AND PASSWORDS

When setting up your Windows 11 computer, understanding the different types of user accounts is crucial for managing access and security. There are three main types of user accounts: Microsoft accounts, local accounts, and guest accounts. A Microsoft account connects you to a range of services like OneDrive, Outlook, and the Microsoft Store. It allows for seamless syncing of settings and files across multiple devices, making it incredibly convenient if you use more than one computer or a smartphone. On the other hand, a local account is specific to your single device and does not offer these syncing capabilities. It is useful if you prefer not to link your activities to an online account. Guest accounts are temporary profiles that allow visitors to use your computer without accessing your personal files. This is particularly helpful if you occasionally have friends or family members using your device.

Creating and managing user accounts in Windows 11 is straight-forward. To start, click on the Start menu and select Settings. Navigate to Accounts and then Family & other users. Here, you'll see options to add new accounts. To create a Microsoft account, click on Add account under the Other users section. You will be prompted to enter an email address or phone number to set up the account. Follow the on-screen instructions to complete the process. For a local account, select I don't have this person's sign-in information, followed by Add a user without a Microsoft account. Enter the username and password, then click Next. Managing account settings and permissions is also done through the Accounts menu. You can change account types, set up parental controls, and adjust other settings to ensure the right level of access for each user.

Setting up secure passwords is an integral part of protecting your accounts. A strong password combines letters, numbers, and special characters to make guessing it difficult. Avoid using easily accessible information like your name or birthdate. Instead, think of a phrase or a combination of unrelated words and add numbers and symbols. For instance, "Blu3$kY!29" is much harder to crack than "password123." Password managers can help you keep track of these complex passwords. These tools store and encrypt your passwords, allowing you to access them easily and securely. Windows 11 has a built-in password manager that you can enable by going to Settings, then Profiles, and selecting Passwords. This feature allows you to save and auto-fill passwords for various websites, reducing the need to remember each one individually.

Account recovery options are essential for regaining access if you forget your password. Setting up security questions is one way to recover your account. During the account setup process, you will be prompted to choose and answer a few security questions. Make sure the answers are something you will remember but not easily guessed by others. Adding a recovery email or phone number provides an additional layer of security. If you forget your password, Microsoft can send a recovery code to your email or phone, allowing you to reset it. To set this up, go to Settings, then Accounts, and select Your info. Under the Security info section, you can add or update your recovery email and phone number.

By understanding the different types of user accounts and setting up secure passwords, you can ensure that your Windows 11 experience is both personalized and secure. Managing accounts and setting up recovery options further enhance your ability to control access and protect your personal information. Whether you're using a Microsoft account for its syncing capabilities or a local account for its simplicity, these steps will help you create a safe and efficient computing environment.

3.5 ENABLING AND USING ACCESSIBILITY FEATURES

Windows 11 is designed to be user-friendly for everyone, including those with visual or physical impairments. The accessibility settings in Windows 11 offer a variety of tools to make your computing experience more comfortable and inclusive. To access these settings, click on the Start menu, select Settings, then navigate to Accessibility. Here, you'll find a range of features aimed at enhancing usability, from screen readers to magnification tools. Each feature is customizable, allowing you to tailor the experience to your specific needs.

For visually impaired users, screen readers can make using a computer much easier. The built-in screen reader in Windows 11 is called Narrator. To enable Narrator, go to the Accessibility settings and select Narrator. Toggle the switch to turn it on. Narrator will start reading aloud the text on your screen, including menus, buttons, and web pages. You can customize Narrator settings to suit your preferences. For example, you can change the voice, adjust the speed and volume, and decide what types of content Narrator should read. This feature is invaluable for those who rely on auditory feedback to navigate their computer.

Magnification tools are another great resource in Windows 11. These tools help enlarge text and images, making them easier to see. To enable the Magnifier tool, go to the Accessibility settings and select Magnifier. Toggle the switch to turn it on. The magnifier will appear on your screen, allowing you to zoom in on specific areas. You can customize the magnifier settings to adjust the zoom level and choose between different magnification modes, such as full screen, lens, or docked. This makes it easier to read small text or view detailed images without straining your eyes.

Speech recognition and dictation are powerful tools for hands-free computing. These features allow you to control your computer and input text using your voice. To set up speech recognition, go to the Accessibility settings and select Speech. Follow the on-screen instructions to train your computer to recognize your voice. Once set up, you can use voice commands to open apps, navigate menus, and perform various tasks. Dictation is another useful feature that lets you convert spoken words into text. To use dictation, press the Windows key + H and start speaking. Your words will appear as text in any text field. This feature is especially helpful for those with limited mobility or those who simply prefer speaking over typing.

Windows 11's accessibility settings are designed to make your computer more usable and enjoyable, regardless of your physical abilities. Whether you need a screen reader to navigate your desktop, a magnifier to read small text, or speech recognition for hands-free control, these tools can significantly enhance your computing experience. By exploring and customizing these features, you can create a digital environment that meets your specific needs and preferences.

In conclusion, personalizing your Windows 11 experience involves more than just aesthetics. By enabling and customizing accessibility features, you can ensure that your computer is tailored to your needs, making it more comfortable and efficient to use. Whether you require visual aids, auditory feedback, or hands-free control, Windows 11 offers a variety of tools to enhance your computing experience.

As you become more comfortable with these features, you'll find that your computer becomes a more natural and intuitive tool. Next, we'll explore how to manage and organize your files effectively, ensuring that your digital workspace is as efficient as possible.

QUIZ: CHAPTER 3 - PERSONALIZING YOUR WINDOWS 11 EXPERIENCE

Questions

1. **How can you set a slideshow as your desktop background in Windows 11?**

   a. Right-click on the desktop and select "Set slideshow."
   b. Go to Settings > Personalization > Background, select "Slideshow," and choose a folder of images.
   c. Open File Explorer and drag images to the desktop.
   d. Use the Start menu to search for "Slideshow mode."

2. **What is the purpose of pinning apps to the taskbar?**

   a. To change the taskbar's color and transparency.
   b. To make apps accessible with a single click.
   c. To hide unused apps from the Start menu.
   d. To arrange apps alphabetically in the taskbar.

3. **Which feature in Windows 11 helps reduce eye strain during late-night use?**

   a. Transparency effects.
   b. High contrast mode.

d. Night light.

e. Dark mode.

4. **What is a Microsoft account's main advantage compared to a local account?**

a. It allows temporary guest access to your device.

b. It syncs settings and files across multiple devices.

c. It eliminates the need for a password.

d. It prevents unauthorized app downloads.

5. **Which accessibility feature reads aloud the text and buttons on your screen?**

a. Magnifier.

b. Narrator.

c. Dictation.

d. Speech recognition.

4

INSTALLING AND MANAGING SOFTWARE

I magine you've just gotten a new computer or updated your current one to Windows 11. Now, you're ready to explore all the amazing apps and tools that can make your digital life easier and more fun. Whether you want to play games, edit photos, or manage your finances, the Microsoft Store is your gateway to a world of applications. This chapter will guide you through finding, installing, and managing apps from the Microsoft Store, ensuring you get the most out of your Windows 11 experience.

4.1 FINDING AND INSTALLING APPS FROM THE MICROSOFT STORE

Accessing the Microsoft Store is your first step to discovering a wide range of applications designed to enhance your Windows 11 experience. To open the Microsoft Store, click on the Start menu at the bottom of your screen (The 4 blue squares). From the menu, you'll see the Microsoft Store icon, which looks like a shopping bag with a Windows logo.

Here is an example. Click on this icon to launch the store. Once opened, you'll be greeted by a clean, organized interface designed for easy navigation. The home screen features sections for promoted apps, essential apps, free games, top free apps, trending apps, and curated collections, making it simple to find something that catches your interest.

Navigating the Microsoft Store is straightforward. At the top of the screen, you'll see tabs for Apps, Games, and Movies & TV shows. Clicking on each tab will take you to a dedicated section to explore different categories. For instance, under Apps, you'll find categories like Productivity, Entertainment, and Education. If you're interested in games, the Games tab showcases various genres such as Action, Puzzle, and Strategy. The Movies & TV shows tab offers a selection of the latest films and TV series available for purchase or rent. This layout ensures you can easily find what you're looking for without feeling overwhelmed.

The Microsoft Store's robust search function makes searching for specific applications easy. At the top of the store interface, you'll find a search bar. Click on it and type in keywords related to the app you're looking for. For example, if you're searching for a photo editing tool, you might enter "photo editor" or the name of a specific app like "Adobe Photoshop." The store will display a list of relevant results. To narrow down your search, use the filters available on the left side of the screen. You can filter results by categories such as age group, type (free, paid, or on sale), and more. This helps you quickly find the most suitable app for your needs.

Once you've found an app that interests you, installing it is a breeze. Click on the app's icon to open its detail page. Here, you'll find important information about the app, including a description, user reviews, ratings, and screenshots. Take a moment to read through this information to ensure the app meets your expectations. When you're ready to install, click the "Get" or "Install" button, depending on whether the app is free or paid. The download and installation process will begin automatically. You can monitor the progress at the top right corner of the store interface, where a small icon will indicate the download status. Once the installation is complete, you can open the app directly from the store or find it in your Start menu.

Managing your installed apps is just as important as finding and installing them. To view and manage the apps you've downloaded, navigate to the "My Library" section of the Microsoft Store. Here is an example of the library icon.

Library

This section is accessible through the profile icon at the top right corner of the store. In "My Library," you'll see a list of all the apps you've installed or purchased. From here, you can launch apps, update them, and manage licenses. Keeping your apps updated ensures you have access to the latest features and security improvements. To check for updates, click on the "Get updates" button in "My Library." If you do not see the update tab in my library then it will be in the download tab, here is what that looks like.

The store will scan for available updates and download them automatically.

By mastering the Microsoft Store, you open up a world of possibilities for your Windows 11 device. Whether you're looking for productivity tools, entertainment apps, or educational software, the store has something for everyone. With a few simple clicks, you can browse, install, and manage a wide variety of applications, making your computing experience richer and more enjoyable.

4.2 INSTALLING SOFTWARE FROM THE INTERNET

Downloading software from the internet can open up endless possibilities for what you can do with your Windows 11 computer. However, it's crucial to understand the importance of downloading software from trusted sources. Reputable websites and official software repositories are your safest options. These sources are more likely to provide software free from malware or unwanted add-ons. Trusted websites typically have clear contact information, digital signatures, and official logos. On the other hand, downloading from unverified or suspicious sites can expose your computer to risks such as viruses, spyware, and other malicious software. These risks can compromise your personal information and the overall performance of your device.

When you're ready to download software, start by navigating to the software's official website. This ensures you're getting the most up-to-date and secure program version. Open your web browser and type the name of the software followed by "official site" into the search bar. For instance, if you're looking to download a program like VLC Media Player, search for "VLC Media Player official site." Click on the link that takes you to the official website. Once there, look for a download link, which is usually prominently displayed on the homepage. Click on the link, and you'll be prompted to save the installer file to your computer. Choose a location that's easy to remember, like your Desktop or Downloads folder.

After downloading the installer file, the next step is to run the installer and follow the installation steps. Locate the installer file you saved—its icon will look like a small box or an executable file. Double-click on the file to open it. A security prompt may appear, asking if you want to allow the program to make changes to your computer. Click "Yes" to proceed. The installer will then open, guiding you through the installation process with on-screen prompts. Read each prompt carefully, as you may be asked to choose installation settings. These settings can include the installation directory, which is the folder where the program will be installed, and additional components you might want or need. It's often best to stick with the default settings unless you have a specific reason to change them.

One of the most common pitfalls when installing software is accidentally agreeing to install unwanted programs or toolbars that are bundled with the main software. These extras can slow down your computer and clutter your system with unnecessary applications. To avoid this, pay close attention to each step of the installation process. Look for checkboxes that offer to install additional software or change your browser settings. These options are usually pre-checked, so you'll need to uncheck them if you don't want the extras. Taking a few extra seconds to read each screen carefully can save you from unwanted clutter and potential security risks.

Downloading software from the internet can be safe and straightforward if you follow these guidelines. Always prioritize trusted websites and take your time during the installation process to avoid unwanted extras. Doing so lets you enjoy the benefits of new software without compromising your computer's security or performance.

4.3 UNINSTALLING AND UPDATING APPLICATIONS

There comes a time when you might find your computer cluttered with applications you no longer use. Uninstalling these applications can free up space and improve your system's performance. To start, click on the Start menu (the 4 blue aquares) and select Settings. From the Settings window, navigate to Apps, then click on Apps & features. Here, you'll see a list of all the installed applications on your computer. Scroll through the list to find the app you want to remove. Click on the app to reveal the Uninstall button. Pressing this button will initiate the uninstallation process. Follow the on-screen prompts to complete the removal. The system will guide you through each step, ensuring that the application is fully uninstalled.

Keeping your applications updated is equally important. Updates often include new features, bug fixes, and security improvements.

To check for updates, you can use the Microsoft Store. Open the Microsoft Store from the Start menu and click on the three-dot menu in the upper right corner. Select Downloads and updates from the dropdown menu. Click on Get updates to scan for available updates for your installed apps. The system will automatically download and install any updates found. Some applications have built-in update features. Open the application, navigate to the Help or Settings menu, and look for an option to check for updates. Following these steps ensures that your applications run smoothly and securely.

For thorough removal of applications, consider using third-party uninstaller tools. These tools can remove residual files and registry entries that the built-in uninstaller might miss. One popular tool is Revo Uninstaller. It performs deep scans to ensure all components of an application are removed. To use Revo Uninstaller, download and install it from a trusted website. Open the tool and select the application you want to uninstall. Follow the prompts to remove the application completely. Other recommended tools include IObit Uninstaller and Geek Uninstaller. These tools are particularly useful for removing stubborn applications that refuse to uninstall through the usual methods.

Managing application updates can be streamlined by enabling automatic updates. In the Microsoft Store, click on the profile icon and select App settings. Toggle the switch for App updates to enable automatic updates. This setting ensures that your apps are always up-to-date without manual intervention. Additionally, some applications allow you to configure update settings within the app itself. Navigate to the Settings or Preferences menu and look for options related to updates. You can set the application to check for updates automatically and notify you when an update is available. Managing these settings helps keep your applications current and reduces the risk of security vulnerabilities.

When you take control of uninstalling and updating your applications, you maintain a clean and efficient system. Whether using built-in tools or third-party uninstallers, these steps ensure your computer remains in optimal condition. Regularly checking for updates and enabling automatic updates keeps your applications running smoothly and securely. By following these guidelines, you can enjoy a hassle-free computing experience, free from unnecessary clutter and outdated software.

4.4 MANAGING DEFAULT APPLICATIONS

When you use your computer, certain tasks automatically open with specific programs. These are known as default applications. For example, when you click on a link, your web browser opens it. Similarly, if you double-click a photo, an image viewer displays it. Setting your preferred default applications ensures that your favorite programs handle these tasks. This can make your computer experience smoother and more enjoyable. Imagine always having your trusted web browser open links or your favorite email client manage your messages.

Changing default applications in Windows 11 is straightforward and gives you control over which programs handle various tasks. To start, open the Settings app by clicking on the Start menu and selecting Settings. From there, navigate to Apps and then Default apps. You'll see a list of categories such as web browser, email, music player, and video player. Clicking on any category will show the current default app and allow you to select a new one from the list of installed applications. For instance, if you prefer using Google Chrome instead of Microsoft Edge, click on Web browser and select Chrome from the list. This change ensures that every time you click on a web link, it opens in Chrome.

File type associations are another aspect of managing default applications. These associations determine which program opens a specific file type, like .jpg for images or .pdf for documents. To manage these associations, stay in the Default apps section of the Settings menu. Scroll down and click on Choose default apps by file type. You'll see a long list of file extensions, each associated with a default application. To change the default app for a specific file type, click on the current app displayed next to the file extension and select a new one from the list. For example, if you want PDF files to open with Adobe Acrobat Reader instead of Microsoft Edge, find the .pdf extension, click on its associated app, and select Adobe Acrobat Reader.

Regularly reviewing and updating your default applications can streamline your computer use and ensure compatibility with the latest software updates. Over time, you might install new applications that better suit your needs, and updating your defaults to reflect these changes can enhance your efficiency. Additionally, software updates often include new features and improvements that can enhance your experience. Periodically checking your default applications ensures that you're using the best tools available. To keep things running smoothly, make it a habit to revisit the Default app settings after installing new software or updates.

Efficiently managing your default applications can significantly enhance your computing experience. Setting your preferred programs for various tasks and file types ensures a seamless and enjoyable interaction with your computer. Regularly reviewing these settings keeps your system optimized and up-to-date, allowing you to focus on what matters most: enjoying your digital activities.

In addition to these steps, you might find it helpful to create a checklist of your preferred applications for different tasks. This can serve as a quick reference whenever you need to update your default settings. A checklist can include categories like web browser, email client, music player, video player, and document editor, along with your chosen applications for each. Having this information readily available lets you easily make adjustments when necessary, ensuring that your computer continues to meet your needs and preferences. Taking the time to manage your default applications effectively can transform your computing experience, making it more intuitive and personalized.

4.5 USING BUILT-IN WINDOWS 11 APPS

Windows 11 comes with a suite of built-in apps that are designed to cover a broad range of everyday tasks. These apps are pre-installed, so you can start using them right away without needing to download anything extra. Among the most useful are Microsoft Edge, Mail, Photos, and Calendar.

Microsoft Edge is the default web browser and is designed for fast, secure, and efficient web browsing. You can use it to access websites, perform searches, and even manage your passwords securely. The browser is built to be user-friendly, offering features like tab grouping and reading mode to enhance your browsing experience. If you're new to Edge, you'll find it easy to navigate with its straightforward interface and helpful features.

The Mail app is another essential tool. It serves as your primary email client, allowing you to manage multiple email accounts in one place. Setting up the Mail app is simple. Open the app, and you'll be prompted to add an email account. You can add accounts from various providers, including Outlook, Gmail, and Yahoo. Enter your email address and password, and follow the on-screen instructions to complete the setup. Once your accounts are added, you can compose and send emails by clicking on the "New mail" button. Organizing your inbox is a breeze with folders and filters. You can create new folders to categorize your emails, making it easy to find important messages. Filters help you automatically sort incoming emails based on criteria like sender or subject.

Photos is an app designed for viewing, editing, and organizing your images. To get started, open the Photos app from the Start menu. You can import photos from your camera or external devices by connecting them to your computer and selecting "Import" within the app. Once your photos are imported, you can view them in the gallery. The app offers basic editing tools such as cropping, applying filters, and adjusting brightness and contrast. These tools are easy to use, even if you're new to photo editing. You can also create albums to group related photos together or make slideshows to share with friends and family. The Photos app keeps everything organized and accessible, making it a valuable tool for managing your image collection.

The Calendar app is perfect for keeping track of your schedule. Open the app, and you'll see a clean, intuitive interface where you can add events and set reminders. To add an event, click on the date and time in the calendar, then enter the event details. You can also set up recurring events for things that happen regularly, like weekly meetings or monthly bill payments. Syncing the Calendar app with other calendars, such as Google Calendar, is straightforward. Go to the settings within the Calendar app, select "Manage accounts," and add your Google account. This ensures all your events are in one place, making it easier to manage your time. The app also offers notifications to remind you of upcoming events, ensuring you never miss an important date.

Each of these built-in apps serves a unique purpose, helping you stay organized and productive. Whether you're browsing the web, managing emails, editing photos, or keeping track of your schedule, Windows 11 has you covered with these essential tools. By taking the time to explore and use these apps, you can greatly enhance your computing experience.

These built-in apps are just the beginning. In the next chapter, we'll dive into advanced customization options and tips to further personalize your Windows 11 experience, ensuring it meets all your needs and preferences.

QUIZ: CHAPTER 4 - INSTALLING AND MANAGING SOFTWARE

Questions

1. **What is the easiest way to find and install apps on Windows 11?**

   a. Downloading apps directly from the internet.
   b. Using a USB drive to transfer apps from another computer.
   c. Browsing and installing apps from the Microsoft Store.
   d. Installing apps from third-party CD-ROMs.

2. **What is a recommended way to avoid installing unwanted programs or toolbars during software installation?**

   a. Always select the default installation settings.
   b. Quickly click through each screen without reading.

c. Carefully review each installation step and uncheck unnecessary options.

d. Install only free programs to avoid unwanted extras.

3. **Where can you find the option to uninstall applications in Windows 11?**

a. In the Recycle Bin.

b. Under Settings > Apps > Apps & features.

c. In the Microsoft Store under "Downloads and updates."

d. By right-clicking the desktop and selecting "Uninstall."

4. **How can you change which program opens a specific file type by default?**

a. Right-click on the file and select "Open with."

b. Go to Settings > Apps > Default apps and choose by file type.

c. Drag the file into a different application.

d. Uninstall the old default app and install a new one.

5. **Which built-in app can help you manage multiple email accounts in one place?**

a. Microsoft Edge

b. Photos

c. Mail

d. Calendar

MASTERING FILE MANAGEMENT

I magine your computer as a big, beautiful library. It holds all your documents, photos, music, and more. But just like a library, it can get cluttered and hard to navigate if things aren't organized properly. Mastering file management is like learning how to be a skilled librarian for your digital world. It helps keep your computer tidy, makes finding files easier, and ensures your important documents are always within reach. In this chapter, we'll explore how to navigate File Explorer, the tool that acts as your personal librarian in Windows 11.

5.1 NAVIGATING FILE EXPLORER

File Explorer is your gateway to everything stored on your computer. Think of it as the main entrance to your digital library. To open File Explorer, click on the File Explorer icon, which looks like a little folder, located on the taskbar at the bottom of your screen. Below is an example.

File Explorer

Another quick way is to use the keyboard shortcut by pressing the Windows key + E. This shortcut instantly brings up File Explorer, saving you a few clicks. You can also access File Explorer by clicking on the Start menu, typing "File Explorer" into the search bar, and then selecting it from the results.

When you open File Explorer, you'll see a window divided into several sections. The main components of this window are the navigation pane, the address bar, and the ribbon toolbar. Below is an example.

The navigation pane is located on the left side of the window. It displays a list of locations and folders, including Quick Access, This PC, and any connected drives or network locations. This pane helps you quickly jump to different parts of your computer without having to navigate through multiple folders. The address bar, found at the top of the window, shows the current path of the folder you're viewing. It's like a map that tells you exactly where you are within your digital library. You can click on any part of the path in the address bar to jump directly to that location.

The ribbon toolbar is located just below the address bar and is packed with useful tools and options. This toolbar is organized into tabs, each containing different commands. The Home tab, for example, includes options for copying, pasting, and deleting files. The View tab allows you to change how your files are displayed, while the Manage tab provides specific tools for the selected item. These tabs help you perform various tasks without having to dig through menus, making File Explorer a powerful tool for managing your files.

Customizing the way you view files in File Explorer can make a big difference in how easily you can find what you're looking for. You can switch between different views to suit your preferences. Icons view offers several sizes: large, medium, and small. Large icons are great for previewing photos, while small icons allow you to see more items at once. List view presents your files in a simple, no-frills list, making it easy to scan through names quickly. Details view provides additional information about each file, such as size, type, and date modified, which can be incredibly useful for sorting and organizing. The preview pane, which you can enable from the View tab, displays a preview of the selected file on the right side of the window. This feature is handy for quickly checking the contents of a document or photo without opening it.

Finding specific files and folders within File Explorer is straight-forward, thanks to the search function. The search bar is located in the upper-right corner of the window. Simply click on it and start typing the name of the file or folder you're looking for. File Explorer will display a list of matching items as you type, helping you find your file quickly. For more precise results, you can use search filters. After entering your search term, click on the Search tab that appears in the ribbon toolbar. Here, you can filter results by date modified, file type, size, and more. Using these filters helps narrow down your search, especially when you have a lot of files with similar names.

Navigating and customizing File Explorer effectively transforms file management from a daunting task into an intuitive process. By understanding the layout, utilizing different views, and mastering the search function, you can keep your digital library organized and accessible, ensuring that you can always find what you need when you need it.

5.2 CREATING AND ORGANIZING FOLDERS

Creating new folders is like adding new shelves to your library, giving you more space to organize your digital books and files. To create a new folder, first open File Explorer. Navigate to the location where you want to create the folder. Once there, you can use the right-click context menu. Right-click on an empty space within the directory, hover over "New," and then select "Folder." A new folder will appear, ready for you to name it. Another way is to use the ribbon toolbar at the top of the File Explorer window. Click on the "Home" tab, then select the "New Folder" button. This method achieves the same result, providing you with a blank folder to name and use.

Naming your folders properly can make all the difference when it comes to finding your files quickly and easily. Use descriptive names that clearly indicate the contents of the folder. For example, instead of naming a folder "Stuff," name it "Vacation Photos 2023" or "Tax Documents 2022." This specificity helps you immediately understand what each folder contains. Avoid using special characters like slashes, colons, or question marks in your folder names, as these can cause issues with file paths and compatibility. Stick to letters, numbers, and spaces, and consider using underscores or hyphens to separate words if needed.

Organizing your folders into a hierarchical structure can further enhance your file management system. Think of it as creating categories and subcategories, much like sections and shelves in a library. Start with high-level categories such as "Work," "Personal," and "Finances." Within each of these main folders, create subfolders for more specific topics. For instance, under "Work," you might have subfolders for "Projects," "Reports," and "Meetings." Within the "Projects" folder, you could have further subfolders for each individual project. This nested folder structure helps keep everything in its place and makes it easier to navigate through your files.

Using color tags and labels adds another layer of organization and makes your folders visually distinctive. Some software, like macOS Finder, allows you to apply color tags to folders and files. While Windows 11 doesn't have this feature built-in, you can still achieve a similar effect with third-party applications like Folder Marker. Applying color tags helps you quickly differentiate between folders at a glance. For example, you might use a red tag for urgent files, a green tag for completed tasks, and a blue tag for ongoing projects. This visual organization makes it easier to manage your files and prioritize your tasks.

Creating and organizing folders effectively ensures that your digital library remains tidy and efficient. By following these steps, you can keep your files easily accessible, reducing the time you spend searching for documents and increasing your productivity. Whether you're organizing family photos, work documents, or personal projects, a well-structured folder system helps you stay on top of your digital life.

5.3 COPYING, MOVING, AND DELETING FILES

Understanding the difference between copying and moving files is key to managing your digital space efficiently. When you copy a file, you create a duplicate that you can place in another location. This means you will have two identical files: one in the original and one in the new locations. Moving a file, on the other hand, changes its location without creating a duplicate. The file is relocated from its original spot to the new one. This is useful when you want to reorganize your files or free up space in a particular folder.

To copy or move files, you have several methods at your disposal. One common way is using drag-and-drop. Open File Explorer and navigate to the file or folder you want to copy or move. To copy, click and hold the file, then drag it to the desired location while holding down the Ctrl key. Release the mouse button to drop the file in the new location. To move the file, click and hold it without pressing any keys, then drag it to the new location and release the mouse button. The file will move to the new spot, leaving the original location empty.

Another method involves using the context menu. Right-click on the file or folder you wish to copy or move. From the menu, select "Copy" to duplicate the file or "Cut" to move it. Navigate to the destination folder, right-click on an empty space, and choose "Paste." The file will appear in the new location. This method is particularly useful if you prefer using menus over dragging and dropping.

Keyboard shortcuts offer a quick and efficient way to copy and move files. To copy a file, select it by clicking on it, then press Ctrl + C. Navigate to the destination folder and press Ctrl + V to paste the duplicate. To move a file, select it and press Ctrl + X to cut it, then go to the new location and press Ctrl + V to paste it. These shortcuts save time and are handy once you get used to them.

Deleting files is just as simple but requires a bit of caution. When you delete a file, it is sent to the Recycle Bin. Below is an example.

The Recycle Bin acts as a safety net, allowing you to recover deleted files if you change your mind. To send a file to the Recycle Bin, right-click on it and select "Delete," or simply press the Delete key on your keyboard. The file will disappear from its original location and move to the Recycle Bin. If you want to restore a deleted file, open the Recycle Bin by double-clicking its icon on the desktop. Find the file you want to recover, right-click on it, and choose "Restore." The file will return to its original location.

Emptying the Recycle Bin permanently deletes all files it contains, freeing up space on your computer. To do this, right-click on the Recycle Bin icon and select "Empty Recycle Bin." Confirm the action when prompted. Be sure you no longer need the files before emptying the Recycle Bin, as this action cannot be undone.

Managing large file transfers can sometimes slow down your computer. To avoid this, consider breaking down large transfers into smaller batches. Instead of moving or copying an entire folder full of files at once, split the contents into smaller groups and transfer them one group at a time. This reduces the load on your system and ensures a smoother process. Using external storage devices, like USB drives or external hard drives, can also help manage large files. Transfer the files to the external device first, then move them to their final destination. This method keeps your computer from becoming bogged down by massive file transfers and provides an additional backup of your files.

5.4 USING EXTERNAL STORAGE DEVICES

Connecting external storage devices like USB drives and external hard drives is a straightforward process, but it's important to do it correctly to avoid data loss or corruption. To begin, locate an available USB port on your computer. Most laptops have these ports on the sides, while desktops usually have them on the front or back. Take your USB drive or external hard drive and gently insert it into the port. Windows 11 should automatically detect the device and display a notification indicating that it's ready to use. If you don't see this notification, open File Explorer and look for the device listed under "This PC."

Properly disconnecting your external storage device is just as important as connecting it. To safely eject the device, click on the small USB icon in the taskbar, usually found on the lower right side of your screen. A menu will appear, listing all connected USB devices. Click on the device you want to eject, and wait for a message that says it's safe to remove the hardware. This step ensures that any data being written to the device is completed, preventing potential data corruption. Once you see the safe-to-remove message, you can physically unplug the device from your computer.

Transferring files to and from external storage devices involves simple actions that you've likely become familiar with. To copy or move files, open File Explorer and navigate to the files you want to transfer. Click and hold the file, then drag it to the external storage device listed in the navigation pane. This action copies the file to the new location. Alternatively, you can right-click on the file, select "Copy" or "Cut" depending on whether you want to duplicate or move the file, then navigate to the external device and right-click to select "Paste." These methods ensure your files are transferred efficiently and accurately.

Keeping your files organized on external storage devices can save you time and frustration. Start by creating folders on the external drive to categorize your files. To create a new folder, right-click on an empty space within the drive, hover over "New," and select "Folder." Name the folder something descriptive, like "Family Photos 2023" or "Work Documents." Avoid using special characters in folder names to prevent compatibility issues. Organizing your files into well-named folders makes it easier to find what you need, especially when dealing with large amounts of data.

Using external storage devices for backups is a reliable way to protect your important files. These devices offer a physical backup that you can easily store in a safe place. To set up automatic backups, you can use Windows 11's built-in tools. Open Settings, go to "Update & Security," and select "Backup." From there, you can add an external drive and configure backup settings to automatically save copies of your files at regular intervals. This automated process ensures your data is always backed up without needing constant attention.

For those who prefer manual backups, the process is equally simple. Connect your external storage device to your computer and open File Explorer. Navigate to the files or folders you want to back up, right-click on them, and select "Copy." Then, go to the external drive and right-click to select "Paste." This manual method allows you to choose exactly which files to back up and when, giving you control over the backup process.

Using external storage devices effectively can greatly enhance your file management system. Whether you're transferring files, organizing data, or setting up backups, these devices offer a flexible and reliable solution for your storage needs.

5.5 BACKING UP IMPORTANT FILES

Backing up your files is like having a safety net for your digital life. Imagine working on an important document for hours only to lose it because of a sudden computer crash. Regular backups protect you against data loss and help you recover quickly from system failures. Think of it as an insurance policy for your data. Without backups, you risk losing precious photos, important documents, and valuable work.

Windows 11 offers built-in tools to make backing up your files straightforward. Two main features are File History and Backup and Restore. File History automatically saves copies of your files in Documents, Music, Pictures, Videos, and Desktop folders. To set up File History, connect an external drive to your computer. Open the Control Panel and navigate to System and Security, then select File History. Click on Turn on to enable it. You can choose how often File History saves copies and how long it retains them. This ensures that you always have recent versions of your files available for recovery.

Backup and Restore is another useful tool that creates system images, allowing you to restore your entire system if something goes wrong. To configure this feature, open the Control Panel and go to System and Security, then Backup and Restore (Windows 7). Click on Set up backup and choose the drive where you want to save your backups. Follow the on-screen instructions to customize your backup settings. You can decide which files to include in the backup and set a schedule for automated backups. This way, you don't have to remember to do it manually.

Using cloud storage services like OneDrive adds another layer of security for your backups. Cloud storage keeps your files safe offsite, protecting them from physical damage to your computer. To set up OneDrive, click on the cloud icon in your taskbar and sign in with your Microsoft account. If you don't see the icon, search for OneDrive in the Start menu. Once signed in, you can choose which folders to sync to the cloud. Files in these folders will automatically upload to OneDrive, making them accessible from any device with internet access. This feature is particularly useful if you travel frequently or use multiple devices.

Setting up a regular backup schedule ensures your data is always protected. Decide whether weekly or monthly backups work best for you, depending on how frequently your files change. Automated backup settings can take the hassle out of this process. For example, in File History, you can set the frequency of backups to every hour, every day, or every week. Similarly, in Backup and Restore, you can schedule regular backups to run at specific times. This consistency means you always have recent copies of your files, minimizing the risk of data loss.

By incorporating these practices into your routine, you safeguard your important files and ensure peace of mind. Regular backups, whether using built-in tools or cloud storage, protect against unforeseen data loss and system failures. In the next chapter, we'll explore how to stay connected with your loved ones and manage your digital communications effectively.

QUIZ: CHAPTER 5 - MASTERING FILE MANAGEMENT

Questions

1. **What is the keyboard shortcut to open File Explorer?**

   a. Ctrl + E
   b. Windows key + E
   c. Alt + F
   d. Ctrl + Shift + F

2. **Which view in File Explorer provides additional details about each file, such as size and date modified?**

   a. Icons view
   b. List view
   c. Details view
   d. Compact view

3. **What is the difference between copying and moving a file?**

   a. Copying creates a duplicate, while moving changes the file's location without creating a duplicate.
   b. Copying removes the file from its original location, while moving leaves it there.
   c. Copying requires an external storage device, while moving doesn't.
   d. Copying only works on certain file types, while moving works on all file types.

4. **What is the purpose of the Recycle Bin?**

a. To permanently delete files without a recovery option.
b. To store deleted files temporarily so they can be recovered if needed.
c. To increase available storage space on the computer.
d. To automatically organize files into folders.

5. **What is the primary function of File History in Windows 11?**

a. To sync files with cloud storage.
b. To create automatic backups of important files.
c. To optimize storage space on your hard drive.
d. To permanently delete files you no longer need.

MAKE A DIFFERENCE WITH YOUR REVIEW

A SMALL ACTION THAT MEANS SO MUCH

"No act of kindness, no matter how small, is ever wasted."

— AESOP

You've just taken a big step in learning Windows 11, and I hope this book has made things easier for you. If it helped you feel more confident using your computer, I'd love to hear about it!

Leaving a review is like sharing a helpful tip with a friend—it lets others know what to expect and helps them decide if this book is right for them. Plus, your feedback helps me improve and create even better guides in the future!

How to Leave a Review

It's quick and easy:

Simply scan the QR code below with your phone and it will take you directly to the review page.

QR code

What to Share

Not sure what to say? Here are some ideas:

- What did you like most about the book?
- Did it help you solve a specific problem?
- Would you recommend it to others who are new to Windows 11?

Your review doesn't have to be fancy—just honest. And I truly appreciate every word!

Thank you for being part of this journey. Your review can help someone else feel confident about learning Windows 11, just like you.

Happy computing!

Gary Moss

6

STAYING CONNECTED WITH EMAIL AND SOCIAL MEDIA

I magine receiving a photo of your grandchild's first steps or an invitation to an old friend's birthday party right in your inbox. Email has made staying connected easier than ever. For many seniors and beginners, email is a gateway to the digital world, offering a simple way to communicate, share, and stay informed. This chapter will guide you through setting up and using email accounts, ensuring you can effortlessly navigate your inbox and make the most of this essential tool.

6.1 SETTING UP AND USING EMAIL ACCOUNTS

Choosing the right email service is the first step in setting up your digital communication hub. Popular email services like Gmail, Outlook, and Yahoo Mail each offer unique features that cater to different needs. Gmail, known for its robust integration with other Google services like YouTube, Google Drive, and Google Docs, provides a seamless experience for users who rely on these tools. Outlook, on the other hand, is part of the Microsoft ecosystem and integrates well with Microsoft Office applications, making it an excellent choice for those who use programs like Word and Excel. Yahoo Mail offers a straightforward, easy-to-use interface, and while it may not have as many integrations as Gmail or Outlook, it remains a reliable option for basic email needs. Each service provides essential features like spam filtering, large storage capacity, and customizable settings, ensuring you can find one that fits your preferences.

Setting up an email account may seem daunting, but it's a straightforward process with the right guidance. Let's start with creating a Gmail account. Navigate to the Gmail sign-up page by typing "Gmail sign up" into your web browser's search bar and selecting the official Google link. Once there, click on "Create account" and choose whether the account is for personal use or business. Fill in your first and last name, then select a username. This will be your email address, so choose something memorable but unique. Next, create a strong password that combines uppercase and lowercase letters, numbers, and special characters. A robust password, such as "Blu3$kY!29," adds an extra layer of security. You'll also be prompted to set up security questions or a recovery email address, which is vital for account recovery if you forget your password. Once you've completed these steps, click "Next" and follow the on-screen instructions to finalize your account setup.

Navigating the email interface is the next step in mastering your new email account. Upon logging into Gmail, you'll find the inbox, which is the main area where incoming emails are displayed. The inbox is organized by date, with the most recent emails at the top. On the left side, you'll see folders like Sent Items, Drafts, and Trash. Sent Items store emails you've sent, Drafts hold messages you're still working on, and Trash contains deleted emails. To compose a new email, click on the "Compose" button, usually found in the upper-left corner. This opens a new window where you can enter the recipient's email address, a subject line, and the body of your message. You can also attach files, such as photos or documents, by clicking the paperclip icon. Once your email is ready, click "Send" to deliver it.

Customizing your email settings can enhance your experience and make managing your inbox more convenient. Gmail, for instance, allows you to change the display theme to suit your preferences. To do this, click on the gear icon in the upper-right corner and select "See all settings." Navigate to the Themes tab, where you can choose from various themes ranging from simple colors to scenic backgrounds. This personalization makes your inbox more visually appealing. Additionally, setting up email notifications ensures you never miss an important message. In the same settings menu, go to the General tab and scroll down to Desktop Notifications. Choose whether you want to be notified of all new emails or only important ones. This feature is particularly useful if you receive a high volume of emails and only want to be alerted for critical messages.

Staying connected through email is a fundamental part of the digital experience. By choosing the right email service, setting up an account, navigating the interface, and customizing your settings, you can ensure that your communication is smooth and efficient. Whether you're catching up with family, making new friends, or managing daily tasks, email provides a reliable and straightforward way to stay in touch.

6.2 MANAGING CONTACTS AND ADDRESS BOOKS

Keeping your contacts organized can make email communication much simpler. An address book helps you manage and keep track of important contacts, ensuring you can find their information quickly when needed. Imagine having all your friends, family, and important services at your fingertips. No more hunting through old emails to find a phone number or email address. A well-organized address book not only saves time but also ensures that you can maintain smooth communication with everyone in your circle.

Adding and editing contacts is straightforward with most email services. Let's start with adding new contacts manually. If you're using Gmail, for instance, open your Gmail account and click on the Google Apps icon (a grid of small squares) in the upper-right corner. Below is an example.

Select Contacts from the dropdown menu. Click on the "Create contact" button and fill in the details such as name, email address, and phone number. Once done, click "Save." Editing existing contact information is just as simple. In your Contacts app, find the contact you want to update, click on their name, then click the pencil icon to edit. Update the necessary information and click "Save." Importing contacts from other services is also possible. For instance, if you have contacts stored in another email account or a CSV file, you can import them into Gmail. Click on the "Import" button, select the file or service, and follow the prompts to complete the process.

Organizing contacts into groups can make communication even more efficient. Creating a new contact group allows you to categorize your contacts based on different criteria, such as family, friends, or work. To create a group in Gmail, navigate to the Contacts app and click on the "Labels" button on the left sidebar. Select "Create label" and name your group. Adding contacts to a group is easy—simply select the contacts you want to include, click on the "Labels" button again, and choose the group you created. This organization makes it easier to send group emails. When composing a new email, type the name of the group in the "To" field, and all members of that group will be added automatically.

Syncing contacts across devices ensures that your address book is always up to date, no matter which device you're using. This feature is particularly useful if you use both a computer and a smartphone. Enabling contact sync on mobile and desktop is usually done through your email account settings. For Gmail, go to Settings on your mobile device, select "Accounts," then "Google," and ensure "Contacts" is toggled on to sync. On your desktop, make sure you're signed into the same Google account in your Contacts app. Troubleshooting sync issues can involve checking your internet connection, ensuring that the sync feature is enabled, and making sure you're signed into the same account on all devices.

By managing your contacts efficiently, you can streamline your communication and make staying in touch with loved ones and important services much easier. A well-organized address book, complete with groups and synced across devices, ensures that you're always prepared to connect with the people who matter most.

6.3 SENDING AND RECEIVING EMAILS WITH ATTACHMENTS

Composing and sending emails is a straightforward process once you get the hang of it. To start, open your email application or web-based email service, such as Gmail or Outlook. Look for the "Compose" button, typically located in the upper-left corner of the inbox. Clicking this button will open a new email window. Here, you'll see fields for the recipient's email address, subject line, and the body of the email. Below is an example

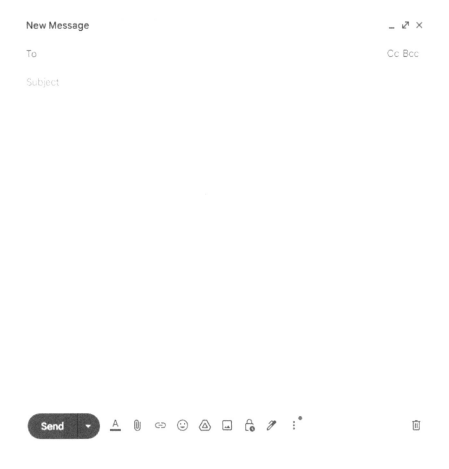

In the "To" field, enter the email address of the person you wish to contact. If you're sending the email to multiple people, separate each email address with a comma. The subject line should be a brief summary of your email's content, helping the recipient understand its purpose at a glance. In the body of the email, write your message. You can use formatting tools like bold, italics, and bullet points to highlight important information. These tools are usually found in a toolbar at the top of the email window. Once your message is complete, review it for any errors or missing information, then click "Send."

Adding attachments to your emails, such as documents, photos, or videos, is equally simple. Look for an attachment icon, often represented by a paperclip, within the email composition window. Clicking this icon will open a file browser, allowing you to navigate through your computer's files. Select the file you wish to attach and click "Open" or "Choose File." The file will then appear as an attachment in your email. If you need to attach multiple files, repeat this process for each one. Many email services also allow you to attach files directly from cloud storage services like Google Drive or OneDrive. This feature is particularly useful for sharing large files that may exceed the email service's size limits. After attaching your files, double-check that they are correctly uploaded before sending your email.

When you receive emails with attachments, it's essential to handle them safely. Open the email and look for the attachments, usually displayed as icons or links near the bottom of the message. Before downloading any attachments, verify the sender's identity to ensure the email is legitimate. If you're unsure, contact the sender through another means to confirm they sent the email. To download an attachment, click on the icon or link. Your browser or email application will prompt you to save the file to your computer. Choose a location where you can easily find the file later, such as the Downloads folder or Desktop. Once downloaded, you can open the attachment by double-clicking it. Common file types include PDFs, Word documents, and image files. Ensure you have the appropriate software installed to open these files. For instance, Adobe Acrobat Reader is needed for PDFs, while Microsoft Word is used for Word documents.

Managing email attachments effectively can help keep your inbox organized and free of clutter. After downloading attachments, consider saving them to specific folders on your computer. For example, create folders for different categories like "Family Photos," "Work Documents," or "Receipts." This organization makes it easier to find files when you need them. Deleting unnecessary attachments from your email is also a good practice. Large attachments can take up significant storage space, potentially causing your inbox to reach its limit. To delete an attachment, open the email and remove the file before deleting the email itself. By regularly managing your attachments, you can maintain a clean and organized inbox, making your email experience more efficient and enjoyable.

6.4 CONNECTING WITH FAMILY AND FRIENDS ON SOCIAL MEDIA

Social media platforms like Facebook, Instagram, and Twitter have revolutionized the way we stay connected with loved ones. Each platform offers unique features tailored to different types of interactions. Facebook, for instance, is perfect for sharing updates, photos, and videos with friends and family. It also has groups and events, making it easy to join communities and stay informed about local happenings. Instagram, known for its visual-centric approach, allows you to share photos and short videos, making it ideal for capturing and sharing moments. Instagram Stories, a feature that lets you post content that disappears after 24 hours, is great for sharing everyday snippets. X, with its character limit on posts, encourages concise communication. It's a fantastic platform for sharing quick updates, news, and engaging in conversations through hashtags.

Creating and setting up social media accounts is straightforward. Let's walk through setting up a Facebook account. Open your web browser and navigate to the Facebook sign-up page by typing "Facebook sign up" into the search bar. Click on the official link. You'll see fields for your first and last name, mobile number or email address, password, date of birth, and gender. Fill in these details carefully, as they help secure your account and make it easier for friends to find you. After completing the form, click "Sign Up." Facebook will send a verification code to your email or mobile number. Enter this code to verify your account. Next, you'll be prompted to choose a profile picture. This can be a recent photo of yourself or any image that represents you. Adjusting privacy settings is crucial to protect your information. Go to the settings menu by clicking the downward-facing arrow in the top-right corner, select "Settings & Privacy," and then "Privacy Checkup." Here, you can control who sees your posts, who can send you friend requests, and how people can find you.

Finding and connecting with family and friends on social media is one of the platform's primary benefits. Use the search bar at the top of the page to type in the name of the person you're looking for. Facebook will display a list of matching profiles. When you find the right one, click on their profile and send a friend request by clicking the "Add Friend" button. On Instagram, you can follow people by searching for their username or full name in the search bar. Once you find their profile, click "Follow" to see their updates in your feed. X works similarly; search for the person's name or username, and click "Follow" to connect with them. These platforms also have suggestions for people you might know, making it easier to expand your network.

Posting updates and sharing content on social media allows you to keep everyone in the loop about your life. On Facebook, start by clicking on the "What's on your mind?" box at the top of your news feed. This opens a new post window where you can type your status update. You can also add photos or videos by clicking the photo/video icon. To tag friends, type the "@" symbol followed by their name. This notifies them of the post and links to their profile. Hashtags, indicated by the "#" symbol, categorize your post and make it discoverable to a broader audience. For instance, adding #FamilyReunion to a post about a family event can connect you with others sharing similar experiences. Instagram follows a similar process. To post, tap the plus sign at the bottom of the screen, select the photo or video you want to share, and add a caption. You can also tag people and use hashtags to increase visibility. Instagram Stories, which you can access by swiping right from the main screen, lets you share photos or videos that disappear after 24 hours. This is great for sharing day-to-day moments without cluttering your main profile. On X, click the "Tweet" button to compose a new tweet. Here, you can type your message, add images, and include hashtags to join broader conversations.

Social media platforms have made it easier than ever to stay connected and engaged with family and friends. By understanding the key features of each platform, setting up your account, finding and connecting with people, and sharing updates, you can make the most of these digital tools to enhance your social life.

6.5 USING VIDEO CALL APPLICATIONS

Video calls have transformed how we stay in touch, bringing faces and voices together no matter the distance. Popular applications like Zoom, Skype, and Microsoft Teams have become household names, each offering unique features to make connecting easier. Zoom is widely known for its user-friendly interface and ability to host large meetings, making it perfect for family gatherings or group chats. Skype is another excellent option, offering both video calling and instant messaging. It's a great choice for one-on-one conversations and smaller group calls. Microsoft Teams, originally designed for business, has also found a place in personal communication. It integrates well with other Microsoft applications, providing a seamless experience for users already familiar with tools like Outlook. Video calling allows you to see expressions, share moments, and feel closer to your loved ones, making it an invaluable tool for maintaining relationships.

Downloading and installing video call applications is straightforward and can be done in just a few steps. To get started with Zoom, go to the official Zoom website or your device's app store. Look for the download button and click it to begin the installation process. Once the download is complete, open the installer and follow the on-screen instructions. You'll be prompted to create an account if you don't already have one. Enter your email address, create a password, and fill in any additional information required. Setting up a profile with a photo and your name helps others recognize you during calls. For Skype, visit the Skype website or app store, download the application, and follow similar steps to install and set up your account. Microsoft Teams can be downloaded from the Microsoft website or app store, and if you already have a Microsoft account, you can use it to sign in. Setting up your profile in Teams is similar, with options to add a photo and personal details.

Initiating and joining video calls involves just a few clicks. In Zoom, you can schedule a meeting by clicking the "Schedule" button on the home screen. Fill in the meeting details, including the date, time, and invitees' email addresses. Once scheduled, Zoom will generate a meeting link that you can share with your contacts. To start an instant meeting, click the "New Meeting" button and invite participants by sharing the meeting ID or link. Joining a call is simple—click on the meeting link you received, or open Zoom and enter the meeting ID provided. Skype and Microsoft Teams follow similar processes. In Skype, click the "Meet Now" button to start a call and share the link with your contacts. To join a call, click the link or enter the meeting code in the Skype interface. Microsoft Teams allows you to schedule meetings through the calendar feature or start an instant meeting by clicking "Meet Now." Joining is as easy as clicking on the invitation link or entering the meeting ID.

Improving your video call experience enhances the quality of your interactions. Ensuring a stable internet connection is crucial. If possible, use a wired connection for better stability. If you're using Wi-Fi, position yourself close to the router to ensure a strong signal. Adjusting camera and microphone settings can also make a significant difference. Position your camera at eye level to create a more natural conversation flow, and ensure your face is well-lit. Test your microphone to ensure clear audio. Most video call applications have settings where you can adjust these features. In Zoom, for example, go to the settings menu and click on "Video" and "Audio" to test and adjust your camera and microphone. Using virtual backgrounds or screen sharing adds a fun and practical element to your calls. Virtual backgrounds allow you to change your backdrop, which can be useful if you're in a cluttered space. In Zoom, click on the "Background & Filters" section in settings to choose a virtual background. Screen sharing lets you share your screen with others, making it easy to show photos, documents, or presentations during the call.

By embracing video call applications, you open up a world of possibilities for staying connected. Whether it's seeing your grandchild's smile, catching up with an old friend, or joining a virtual meeting, these tools bring people closer together despite physical distances. As we continue to navigate the digital age, mastering these applications ensures that you remain connected, engaged, and involved in the lives of those you care about.

In the next chapter, we'll explore how to enhance security and privacy while using your computer, ensuring that your online activities remain safe and secure.

QUIZ: CHAPTER 6 - STAYING CONNECTED WITH EMAIL AND SOCIAL MEDIA

Questions

1. **What is a popular feature of Gmail that makes it a strong choice for many users?**

   a. Integration with Microsoft Office
   b. Integration with Google services like Google Drive and Google Docs
   c. Built-in video calling
   d. Large video streaming capabilities

2. **Which folder in Gmail contains messages that you started but haven't sent yet?**

   a. Trash
   b. Sent Items
   c. Drafts
   d. Inbox

3. **What is the purpose of organizing contacts into groups in an email address book?**

a. To prevent contacts from syncing across devices
b. To categorize contacts for easier email communication
c. To automatically delete unused contacts
d. To ensure contacts are not duplicated

4. **What is one of the main advantages of using social media platforms like Facebook or Instagram?**

a. They are completely ad-free.
b. They allow you to quickly connect and share updates with friends and family.
c. They can replace all email communications.
d. They provide built-in virus protection.

5. **What is a helpful practice when receiving emails with attachments?**

a. Download every attachment without verifying the sender.
b. Verify the sender's identity before downloading the attachment.
c. Delete attachments immediately after receiving them.
d. Automatically forward all attachments to a new email account.

7

ENHANCING SECURITY AND PRIVACY

I magine you're settling in for a cozy evening with your favorite book, knowing your doors are securely locked. In the same way, safeguarding your computer ensures peace of mind while you explore the digital world. Windows 11 offers robust security features to protect your device, and understanding these tools is the first step in creating a secure environment. This chapter focuses on setting up Windows Defender and other antivirus software to keep your computer safe from various online threats.

7.1 SETTING UP WINDOWS DEFENDER AND ANTIVIRUS SOFTWARE

Windows Defender is your computer's built-in security guard, always on the lookout for potential threats. This powerful tool comes pre-installed with Windows 11, offering real-time protection against viruses, spyware, ransomware, and hackers. Real-time protection means that Windows Defender actively monitors your system for malicious activity and takes immediate action to neutralize threats. This constant vigilance ensures that your computer remains protected even as you browse the web, download files, or open emails.

To get started with Windows Defender, you'll need to access Windows Security. Click on the Start menu, then select Settings. Navigate to Update & Security and click on Windows Security. Here, you'll find various security options, including Virus & threat protection. Click on this option to open the main Windows Defender interface. Ensure that real-time protection is turned on. This feature automatically scans files and programs as they are accessed, providing an essential layer of defense. Additionally, you can configure scan options to suit your needs. Quick scans check common locations where malware typically hides, while full scans examine all files and programs on your hard drive. If you have specific concerns, a custom scan allows you to target particular folders or external drives.

Regular scans are a cornerstone of maintaining your computer's security. Scheduling scans ensure that your system is routinely checked for threats without requiring manual intervention. In the Windows Defender interface, click on Virus & Threat Protection settings. Scroll down to find Scan options. Here, you can set up scheduled scans to run daily, weekly, or monthly at a time that suits you. To run a manual scan, simply select Quick Scan, Full Scan, or Custom Scan, and click Scan Now. Regular scans help identify and remove any threats that may have slipped through real-time protection, keeping your system clean and secure.

While Windows Defender provides robust protection, adding a third-party antivirus can offer additional security layers. Several reputable programs, such as Norton Antivirus, McAfee, and Bitdefender, provide excellent protection against a wide range of threats. Norton Antivirus is known for its extra security features, such as Data Protector for ransomware protection and online backup. McAfee excels in single-PC households, offering a simple firewall and virus protection pledge. Bitdefender is highly rated for its multi-layered ransomware protection and secure browser for online banking. Installing a third-party antivirus is straightforward. Visit the official website of the antivirus software you choose, download the installer, and follow the prompts. Ensure you configure the settings to enable real-time protection and schedule regular scans, just as you did with Windows Defender.

Incorporating these security measures into your routine ensures that your computer remains a safe space for your digital activities. Regular scans, real-time protection, and the added layer of a third-party antivirus provide comprehensive security, giving you the confidence to explore the digital world without worry.

7.2 CONFIGURING PRIVACY SETTINGS

Privacy settings are a critical part of your digital life, protecting your personal information from prying eyes. Not managing these settings can expose you to risks such as targeted advertising, data breaches, and unauthorized access to your location and activities. Enhanced privacy settings, on the other hand, help you control what information is shared, who sees it, and how it's used, providing peace of mind as you navigate the internet and use various apps.

To adjust your privacy settings in Windows 11, start by clicking on the Start menu and selecting Settings. From there, navigate to Privacy & Security. Here, you'll find a variety of options to manage your privacy. One of the first areas to look at is app permissions. These settings control which apps can access your location, camera, and microphone. Select Location under the App permissions section. You'll see a toggle switch to turn location services on or off. If you prefer not to share your location, you can turn this off entirely. However, some apps, like maps, may require location access to function correctly. To manage location access for individual apps, scroll down to the list of apps and toggle permissions on or off based on your preferences.

Next, move on to managing permissions for your camera and microphone. These settings are crucial for apps that require video or audio input, such as video call applications. In the Privacy & Security settings, select Camera and review which apps have access. Toggle off any permissions for apps that don't need camera access. Repeat the process for the Microphone to ensure only trusted applications can use it. Configuring these settings helps prevent unauthorized apps from accessing your camera and microphone, reducing the risk of eavesdropping or unwanted recordings.

General privacy options are also worth exploring. These settings include controls for your advertising ID, which is used to personalize ads based on your activity, and diagnostic data, which sends information to Microsoft to help improve their services. In the Privacy & Security settings, click on General. Here, you can toggle off options like "Let apps use advertising ID to make ads more interesting to you" to reduce personalized advertising. Under Diagnostics & feedback, you can choose whether to send optional diagnostic data to Microsoft. Opting out enhances your privacy by limiting the amount of data shared with Microsoft.

Location settings are another important aspect of privacy management. Controlling your location services can protect your privacy, especially if you're concerned about apps tracking your movements. In the Location settings, you can turn off location services entirely or manage them on a per-app basis. For instance, you might allow your weather app to access your location for accurate forecasts but deny access to other apps that don't need this information. This selective control ensures that only essential apps can use your location data.

Maintaining online privacy goes beyond configuring settings on your computer. Using a **virtual private network** (VPN) can significantly enhance your online privacy. A VPN encrypts your internet connection, making it difficult for others to track your online activities. Many VPN services are available, both free and paid. Choose one that suits your needs and follow their setup instructions to start browsing securely. Additionally, regularly clearing your browsing history and cookies can help maintain your privacy. Browsing history stores a record of the websites you visit, while cookies track your online behavior. To clear these, open your web browser, go to the settings menu, and find the options for clearing browsing data. Select the data types you want to delete and confirm the action. Regularly clearing this data reduces the amount of information websites can collect about you.

By carefully configuring your privacy settings and adopting good online privacy habits, you create a safer and more secure digital environment. This proactive approach helps protect your personal information, giving you greater control over your digital life.

7.3 RECOGNIZING AND AVOIDING ONLINE SCAMS

As you navigate the internet, it's crucial to be aware of online scams designed to trick you into giving away personal information or money. One common scam is phishing, where scammers send emails or create websites that look like they come from reputable organizations. These messages often urge you to click on a link or download an attachment. Another scam involves fake tech support calls. Scammers pose as technical support agents, claiming your computer has a virus and asking for remote access or payment for unnecessary services. Lottery and prize scams are also prevalent, where you receive emails or messages claiming you've won a prize but must pay a fee or provide personal information to claim it.

Recognizing phishing attempts is your first line of defense. Always check the sender's email address carefully. Scammers often use addresses that look similar to legitimate ones but have slight differences. Avoid clicking on links or downloading attachments from unknown sources. These can lead you to malicious websites or infect your computer with malware. Pay attention to the language used in the email. Phishing emails often contain urgent or threatening language, such as "Your account will be suspended unless you verify your information immediately." Legitimate companies rarely use such tactics.

To stay safe, never share personal information like passwords or credit card numbers via email. If you receive a suspicious email, verify its legitimacy by contacting the company directly using known contact information, not the details provided in the email. Be cautious with unsolicited communication, especially if it asks for personal information or payments. Scammers often create a sense of urgency to pressure you into making quick decisions. Take your time to verify any requests you receive.

If you believe you have been targeted by a scam, take immediate action to protect yourself. Report the scam to the authorities, such as the Federal Trade Commission (FT or your local consumer protection agency. This helps prevent others from falling victim to the same scam. Change your passwords right away, especially if you provide any personal information. Use a combination of letters, numbers, and symbols to create strong passwords. Additionally, enable two-factor authentication (2F on your accounts for an extra layer of security.

Running a security scan on your computer can help identify and remove any malware that may have been installed. Use your antivirus software to perform a full scan. If you don't have antivirus software, consider downloading a reputable program like Norton, McAfee, or Bitdefender. These programs offer comprehensive protection and can help keep your computer secure.

Scammers continually come up with new tactics, so staying informed and vigilant is key. Understanding the types of online scams and recognizing the signs can significantly reduce your risk of falling victim. By following these practical steps, you can navigate the internet with confidence, knowing you have the tools to protect yourself.

7.4 MANAGING PASSWORDS AND TWO-FACTOR AUTHENTICATION

Imagine the front door to your home had a flimsy lock that could be easily picked. You wouldn't feel safe, right? The same principle applies to your online accounts. Strong passwords are the first line of defense, protecting your personal information from unauthorized access. Weak passwords, such as "123456" or "password," are like that flimsy lock—they can be guessed easily, putting your data at risk. On the other hand, strong, unique passwords act like robust locks, making it much harder for cybercriminals to break in. The benefits of using strong passwords include better security, less risk of identity theft, and greater peace of mind.

Creating strong passwords involves a few key practices. First, use a mix of letters, numbers, and symbols. This combination makes your password harder to crack. Avoid using common words and phrases, as these are often the first things hackers try. Instead, opt for passphrases—strings of random words that are easy for you to remember but difficult for others to guess. For instance, "BlueSky!42$Tree" is a strong passphrase. It's long, includes different character types, and avoids common words. Remember, the longer and more complex your password, the stronger it is.

Password managers are incredibly useful tools that simplify the process of maintaining strong, unique passwords for all your accounts. These tools store and encrypt your passwords, allowing you to access them easily and securely. Examples of reliable password managers include LastPass, Dashlane, and 1Password. To set up a password manager, download the software from the provider's official website, create a master password, and start adding your accounts. The master password is the only one you need to remember, as it unlocks the vault containing all your other passwords. Most password managers also offer features like password generation, which creates strong, random passwords for you, and auto-fill, which enters your login credentials automatically when you visit a website. This not only enhances security but also saves time, as you no longer need to remember or type out each password manually.

Two-factor authentication (2F adds an additional layer of security to your accounts. With 2FA, you need to provide two pieces of information to log in: your password and a second factor, usually a code sent to your phone or generated by an authentication app. This means that even if someone manages to steal your password, they still can't access your account without the second factor. To enable 2FA, go to the security settings of your online accounts. Look for options like "Two-factor authentication," "2-step verification," or "Multi-factor authentication." Follow the instructions to link your phone number or set up an authentication app such as Google Authenticator or Authy. Once set up, you'll receive a code each time you log in, adding a significant hurdle for anyone trying to access your account without permission.

Using an authentication app is straightforward. After downloading the app to your smartphone, open it and follow the setup instructions. Typically, you'll scan a QR code provided by the service you're securing, which links the app to your account. When you log in, open the app to retrieve the six-digit code it generates. Enter this code along with your password to gain access. Authentication apps generate new codes every 30 seconds, ensuring that each code is unique and time-sensitive. This dynamic nature makes 2FA highly effective at preventing unauthorized access.

By employing strong passwords, utilizing a password manager, and enabling two-factor authentication, you significantly enhance your online security. These practices help protect your personal information from cyber threats, ensuring that your digital life remains secure.

7.5 SAFE PRACTICES FOR ONLINE SHOPPING AND BANKING

When you shop or bank online, secure transactions are vital. They protect your personal and financial information from online fraud and identity theft. The internet offers convenience, but it also exposes you to risks. Fraudsters can intercept your data or trick you into sharing sensitive information. Following safe online practices can protect you from these dangers and ensure your transactions remain secure.

Identifying secure websites is a fundamental step in safe online transactions. Always look for "HTTPS" at the beginning of the website URL. The "S" stands for secure, indicating that the site uses encryption to protect your data. You should also see a padlock icon next to the URL. Clicking on this icon will provide more details about the site's security certificate. Trust seals, like those from Norton or McAfee, are also good indicators of a website's security. These seals often link to verification pages that confirm the site's legitimacy. Avoid sites without these security markers, especially if they request personal or payment information.

When shopping online, stick to reputable websites and sellers. Well-known retailers like Amazon, Best Buy, and Walmart are generally safe bets. If you're buying from a smaller retailer or an individual seller, do some research first. Look for reviews and ratings from other customers. This can give you a sense of the seller's reliability. Public Wi-Fi is convenient, but it's not secure. Avoid making transactions over public networks, as they are more susceptible to hacking. Instead, use a secure home network or a trusted mobile data connection. Regularly monitor your bank statements for any suspicious activity. Early detection of unauthorized transactions can prevent further damage and make it easier to resolve issues with your bank.

Setting up and using online banking safely involves a few essential steps. First, create strong passwords for your banking accounts. Use a mix of letters, numbers, and symbols to enhance security. Enable two-factor authentication (2F if your bank offers it. This adds an extra layer of protection by requiring a second form of verification, usually a code sent to your phone, in addition to your password. Always log out of your online banking session when you're done. This ensures that no one else can access your account if you leave your computer unattended. Most banks also offer alerts for transactions, which can help you keep track of your account activity in real-time.

In conclusion, understanding and practicing safe online shopping and banking habits are crucial for protecting your personal and financial information. By recognizing secure websites, choosing reputable sellers, avoiding public Wi-Fi, and regularly monitoring your statements, you can significantly reduce the risks. Setting up strong passwords, enabling two-factor authentication, and logging out after each session further enhance your security. These measures ensure that your online transactions remain safe, allowing you to enjoy the convenience of the digital world without compromising your security.

QUIZ: CHAPTER 7 - ENHANCING SECURITY AND PRIVACY

1. **What is one of the primary benefits of Windows Defender's real-time protection?**

a. It prevents you from downloading any files.
b. It only scans your system on-demand.
c. It monitors your system continuously and neutralizes threats immediately.
d. It disables other antivirus software.

2. **Which setting can be adjusted to limit apps' access to your location, camera, and microphone?**

a. Privacy & Security > App permissions
b. Windows Update > Advanced options
c. Accessibility > Display settings
d. Network & Internet > Data usage

3. **What is the best practice when receiving an email that appears to be from a known organization but asks for sensitive information?**

a. Provide the information immediately.
b. Verify the email's legitimacy by contacting the organization through known contact details.
c. Click on any provided links to verify the email's authenticity.
d. Delete the email without checking its validity.

4. **What is the purpose of using two-factor authentication (2F?**

a. To store your passwords securely.
b. To automatically block suspicious websites.
c. To add an extra layer of security by requiring a second form of verification.
d. To prevent all online purchases.

5. **What should you look for to ensure a website is secure for online shopping?**

a. The site loads very quickly.
b. HTTPS in the URL and a padlock icon.
c. The website displays bright colors and graphics.
d. It has a long, complicated web address.

8

CONNECTING AND USING PERIPHERAL DEVICES

I magine trying to write a letter without a pen or pencil. Just as these tools are essential for putting words on paper, peripheral devices like printers and scanners are crucial for getting the most out of your computer. These devices help you complete a variety of tasks, from printing important documents to digitizing old family photos. In this chapter, we will guide you through the process of setting up and using these peripherals, ensuring you can easily connect, configure, and utilize them to their full potential.

8.1 SETTING UP PRINTERS AND SCANNERS

Connecting a printer or scanner to your Windows 11 computer might seem daunting, but it's a straightforward process once you know the steps. For wired printers and scanners, start by locating the USB cable that came with your device. Plug one end into the printer or scanner and the other end into an available USB port on your computer. Windows 11 usually recognizes the device automatically and installs the necessary drivers. If it doesn't, don't worry; we'll cover how to manually install drivers shortly.

Setting up a wireless printer involves a few more steps but offers the convenience of printing from anywhere within your Wi-Fi network's range. Begin by turning on the printer and ensuring it's connected to the same Wi-Fi network as your computer. On your computer, go to Start > Settings > Bluetooth & devices > Printers & scanners. Click "Add a printer or scanner" and wait for your computer to find nearby printers. Once your printer appears on the list, select it and click "Add device." If your printer supports WPS (Wi-Fi Protected Setup), you can use this feature for an even easier setup. Press the WPS button on your router, then press the corresponding WPS button on your printer. This will automatically connect the printer to your network without needing to enter a Wi-Fi password.

Now, let's talk about installing printer and scanner drivers. Drivers are software that allows your computer to communicate with your peripheral devices. Sometimes, Windows 11 will not automatically find the correct drivers, especially for older or less common devices. In such cases, you'll need to visit the manufacturer's website. Look for a section labeled "Support" or "Downloads." Enter your device's model number, and download the driver that matches your operating system. Once downloaded, open the file and follow the on-screen instructions to install the driver. This process typically involves agreeing to a license agreement and confirming installation locations.

After successfully connecting and installing your printer or scanner, it's time to configure its settings. To access the Devices and Printers section, open the Control Panel and select "Devices and Printers." Here, you'll see icons for all connected printers and scanners. Right-click on your printer's icon and select "Set as default printer" to make it your primary printing device. Next, right-click again and choose "Printing preferences." This opens a window where you can adjust print quality, paper size, and other settings. For instance, you might want to change the print quality to "High" for important documents or photographs, or switch to grayscale to save on color ink.

Scanning documents and photos is equally straightforward. Windows 11 includes a built-in tool called the Windows Scan app. Open the Start menu and type "Scan" to find and open the app. Place your document or photo on the scanner bed, then select your scanner from the list of available devices in the app. Choose the file type (such as JPEG or PDF) and the resolution for the scan. Higher resolutions result in better image quality but larger file sizes. Click "Preview" to see a low-resolution scan of your document, and adjust settings if needed. Once satisfied, click "Scan" to start the process. The scanned file will be saved to a folder of your choice. If you prefer, you can use the manufacturer's software, which often includes additional features like automatic color correction and advanced file management.

For those who need to convert scanned documents to PDF, many scanners' software packages offer this feature directly. Alternatively, you can use free online tools or software like Adobe Acrobat. Simply upload the scanned images and choose the "Convert to PDF" option. This is particularly useful for creating digital archives of important documents, making them easy to store and share.

Connecting and configuring printers and scanners may seem complex, but with these steps, you'll find the process manageable and rewarding. These devices enhance your computer's functionality, allowing you to complete a wide range of tasks efficiently.

8.2 USING EXTERNAL HARD DRIVES AND USB DEVICES

Connecting external hard drives and USB devices to your Windows 11 computer is a straightforward process that significantly enhances your data storage capabilities. To start, locate an available USB port on your computer. Plug one end of the USB cable into the external hard drive or USB device, and the other end into the computer's USB port. Your computer should recognize the device automatically. A notification will pop up, indicating that the device is ready for use. If you don't see this notification, open File Explorer by clicking the folder icon on your taskbar or pressing Windows key + E. Your external device should appear under "This PC" as a new drive.

Safely ejecting devices is crucial to prevent data loss. Before unplugging your device, ensure no files are being transferred. Click the "Safely Remove Hardware and Eject Media" icon in the taskbar, usually found near the clock. Select your device from the list, and wait for the notification that says it's safe to remove the hardware. For those using laptops, this step is especially important as sudden disconnections can corrupt files or damage the drive. If you don't see the eject icon, you can also safely eject the device through File Explorer by right-clicking on the drive and selecting "Eject."

Once your external device is connected, managing files becomes a breeze. Open File Explorer and click on the external drive listed under "This PC." You'll see a window displaying the contents of your device. You can navigate through folders just like you would on your main hard drive. To copy files from your computer to the external device, select the files you want to transfer, right-click, and choose "Copy." Then, navigate to the external drive, right-click again, and select "Paste." Moving files works similarly, but instead of copying, choose "Cut" to remove the files from their original location. This method is useful for freeing up space on your computer while keeping your important files accessible.

Creating and organizing folders on your external device helps keep everything tidy. In the File Explorer window for your external drive, right-click on an empty space, hover over "New," and select "Folder." Name the folder descriptively, such as "Vacation Photos" or "Tax Documents." Drag and drop files into these folders to keep them organized. This hierarchical structure makes it easier to find what you need quickly. If your device starts to fill up, organizing files into folders can also help you identify which items can be deleted or transferred elsewhere.

Backing up important files to an external device is a smart way to protect your data. You can manually copy files to your external drive by following the steps mentioned earlier. However, setting up automatic backups ensures that your files are regularly updated without requiring manual intervention. Windows 11 includes built-in tools for this purpose. Open the Start menu, type "Backup settings," and select "Backup using File History." Connect your external drive, and Windows will prompt you to set it as your backup destination. Follow the on-screen instructions to configure which folders to back up and how frequently the backups should occur. This automated process provides peace of mind, knowing that your data is safely stored.

Formatting an external storage device prepares it for use with your computer and can resolve issues with incompatible file systems. To format your drive, open File Explorer, right-click on the external drive, and select "Format." A window will appear with several options. Choose the appropriate file system: NTFS is ideal for Windows-only environments, while exFAT is suitable if you plan to use the drive with both Windows and macOS. Perform a quick format for a faster process, or a full format for a thorough clean that checks for bad sectors. Be aware that formatting will erase all data on the drive, so ensure you've backed up any important files beforehand. This step is essential for maintaining a clean and functional storage device.

Connecting and using external hard drives and USB devices expands your computer's capabilities, offering additional storage and backup solutions. By following these steps, you can ensure your devices are set up correctly, and your data remains organized and secure.

8.3 CONNECTING TO BLUETOOTH DEVICES

Bluetooth technology is a marvel of modern computing, allowing you to connect various devices wirelessly. Imagine sitting at your desk and using a wireless keyboard, freeing your workspace from the clutter of cables. Bluetooth facilitates this kind of seamless communication between devices. It uses radio waves to transfer data over short distances, typically up to 30 feet. Common Bluetooth devices include mice, keyboards, headphones, and even some printers and scanners. These devices communicate with your computer through a Bluetooth adapter, either built-in or added via a USB dongle.

To enable Bluetooth on your Windows 11 computer, start by accessing the settings. Click on the Start menu, then select Settings, followed by Bluetooth & devices. Here, you'll see a toggle switch to turn Bluetooth on or off. Slide this switch to the "On" position. Once Bluetooth is enabled, your computer will start searching for nearby Bluetooth devices. This is the first step towards pairing your devices and enjoying the convenience of wireless technology.

Pairing a Bluetooth device involves a few straightforward steps. First, put the Bluetooth device into pairing mode. This usually involves holding down a specific button until an indicator light flashes. For example, on a Bluetooth mouse, you might need to press and hold the power button. Once the device is in pairing mode, return to your computer. In the Bluetooth settings, click on "Add device" and wait for your computer to discover the available Bluetooth devices. When your device appears on the list, select it and follow any additional instructions to complete the pairing process. This might include entering a passcode or simply confirming the connection. Once paired, your device will be ready to use.

Managing Bluetooth settings is essential for maintaining a smooth connection. To remove a paired device, go back to the Bluetooth & devices settings. Find the device you want to remove, click on it, and select "Remove device." This action unpairs the device, freeing up space for other devices. Renaming your Bluetooth devices can make it easier to identify them, especially if you have multiple devices connected. Click on the device name and select "Rename." Enter a new name that helps you recognize the device quickly, like "John's Headphones" or "Office Keyboard."

Checking the battery levels of connected Bluetooth devices is another useful feature in Windows 11. For devices like keyboards and mice, knowing the battery level helps prevent unexpected disconnections. In the Bluetooth & devices settings, select the device, and if it supports battery level reporting, you'll see the current battery status. This allows you to recharge or replace batteries before they run out, ensuring continuous use.

Bluetooth troubleshooting is occasionally necessary when connections become unstable. If a device stops working, try turning Bluetooth off and on again. This simple step often resolves minor issues. If problems persist, remove the device and pair it again. Ensure that the device is within the effective range and that there are no significant obstacles, like walls, between the device and your computer. Interference from other wireless devices can also affect Bluetooth performance, so try to keep other electronic devices away from your Bluetooth peripherals.

Bluetooth technology enhances your computing experience by providing the flexibility and convenience of wireless connections. Whether you're using a wireless keyboard to type or Bluetooth headphones to listen to music, understanding how to connect and manage these devices ensures you get the most out of your technology. With these steps, you can easily enable, pair, and manage Bluetooth devices on your Windows 11 computer, making your digital life more efficient and clutter-free.

8.4 MANAGING CONNECTED DEVICES IN WINDOWS 11

When you have multiple devices connected to your computer, managing them efficiently becomes crucial. Windows 11 provides a convenient way to view and manage all your connected devices through the Devices and Printers section. To access this, open the Control Panel by clicking on the Start menu and typing "Control Panel" in the search bar. Select "Control Panel" from the search results. Once in the Control Panel, click on "Devices and Printers." This section displays all your connected devices, including printers, scanners, Bluetooth devices, and external drives. Each device is represented by an icon, making it easy to identify and manage them.

In the Devices and Printers interface, you have several options for managing your devices. For example, you can set a default printer by right-clicking on the printer icon and selecting "Set as default printer." This ensures that all your print jobs are directed to this printer unless you specify otherwise. You can also change device properties and settings by right-clicking on the device icon and selecting "Properties." This opens a new window where you can adjust various settings, such as device name, location, and additional preferences. For printers, you might find options to change print quality, paper type, and other detailed settings that can enhance your printing experience.

Ensuring that your connected devices have the latest drivers installed is essential for smooth operation. Outdated or missing drivers can lead to performance issues and connectivity problems. To check for driver updates, open the Device Manager by right-clicking on the Start menu and selecting "Device Manager." In the Device Manager window, you'll see a list of all hardware components and connected devices. Locate the device for which you want to update the driver, right-click on it, and select "Update driver." Choose the option to search automatically for updated driver software. Windows will search online for the latest drivers and install them if available. If Windows cannot find the driver, visit the manufacturer's website, download the appropriate driver for your model, and follow the installation instructions.

Removing devices you no longer use helps keep your system organized and can prevent potential conflicts. To remove a device, go back to the Devices and Printers section in the Control Panel. Right-click on the device you wish to remove and select "Remove device." Confirm the action, and Windows will disconnect and remove the device from the list. This cleaning process ensures that only active and necessary devices are connected, reducing clutter and potential issues.

Troubleshooting common device issues can often be done using built-in Windows tools. If a device isn't working correctly, first check the connections. Ensure that all cables are securely plugged in and that wireless devices have a strong signal. Sometimes, simply restarting the computer and the device can resolve minor issues. If the problem persists, use the Windows Troubleshooter tool. Go to Settings > Update & Security > Troubleshoot. Select the type of device you're having trouble with, such as a printer or Bluetooth device, and run the troubleshooter. Windows will attempt to diagnose and fix the issue automatically. If the troubleshooter cannot resolve the problem, it may provide suggestions for further steps.

For more complex issues, checking device properties and settings can provide additional insights. In the Devices and Printers section, right-click on the device and select "Properties." Review the settings and make sure everything is configured correctly. Sometimes, adjusting a small setting can resolve the issue. For example, if a printer is showing as offline, checking the network settings and ensuring it's connected to the same Wi-Fi network as your computer can bring it back online.

Managing connected devices in Windows 11 becomes straightforward with these tools and steps. By regularly updating drivers, configuring settings, and using troubleshooting tools, you can ensure that all your devices work seamlessly with your computer. This proactive approach helps maintain an efficient and organized digital workspace, allowing you to focus on your tasks without the hassle of technical issues.

8.5 TROUBLESHOOTING PERIPHERAL DEVICE ISSUES

Peripheral devices, whether they are printers, scanners, keyboards, or external drives, can sometimes present issues that interrupt your workflow. Imagine plugging in your new printer only to find that your computer doesn't recognize it. This is a common problem and can be quite frustrating. There are several typical issues users often encounter with external devices, such as the device not being recognized, connection problems, or driver-related issues. These problems can usually be resolved with some basic troubleshooting steps.

When your device is not recognized, the first step is to check the physical connections. Ensure that the cables are securely plugged in and that there are no signs of damage. A loose or frayed cable can prevent the device from establishing a proper connection. If you're using a wireless device, check that it's within range and that there are no significant obstacles between the device and your computer. Sometimes, simply unplugging the device and plugging it back in can solve the problem. Another useful step is to restart both your computer and the device. This can refresh the system and re-establish the connection. If the issue persists, try connecting the device to a different USB port or even another computer to determine if the problem lies with the device or the port.

Driver problems are another common issue. Drivers are software that allow your computer to communicate with peripheral devices. If a driver is outdated, missing, or corrupted, the device won't function correctly. To check for driver issues, open the Device Manager by right-clicking on the Start menu and selecting "Device Manager." Look for any devices with a yellow exclamation mark, which indicates a driver problem. Right-click on the device and select "Update driver." Choose the option to search automatically for updated driver software. If Windows can't find the driver, visit the manufacturer's website to download the latest driver for your device. Follow the installation instructions provided on the website. If the problem persists, try uninstalling the driver from the Device Manager and then reinstalling it.

Windows 11 includes a built-in Troubleshooter tool that can help diagnose and fix common device issues. To access the Troubleshooter, go to Settings > Update & Security > Troubleshoot. You'll see a list of available troubleshooters for different types of devices, such as printers or Bluetooth devices. Select the appropriate troubleshooter and click "Run the troubleshooter." Windows will attempt to identify and resolve the issue. This tool is handy for addressing problems that aren't immediately obvious, such as software conflicts or minor configuration errors. It guides you through a series of steps and provides solutions based on the detected issue.

If basic troubleshooting steps don't resolve the problem, it might be time to seek additional help. Contacting the device manufacturer's support team is a good place to start. They can provide specific guidance for your device and may offer solutions not covered in standard troubleshooting guides. Additionally, online forums and communities can be valuable resources. Websites like Microsoft's support forum or manufacturer-specific forums often have discussions about similar issues, with solutions provided by other users or experts. Reading through these forums can provide insights and potential fixes that you might not have considered. If you're still unable to resolve the issue, consulting a professional technician can be the best course of action. Technicians have the expertise and tools to diagnose and fix more complex problems, ensuring that your device functions correctly.

By following these troubleshooting steps, you can often resolve peripheral device issues on your own, saving time and avoiding frustration. From checking physical connections to updating drivers and using the Windows Troubleshooter, these methods provide a solid foundation for addressing common problems. When these steps aren't enough, seeking help from the manufacturer or a professional ensures that your devices continue to work smoothly, enhancing your overall computing experience.

Understanding these troubleshooting techniques will empower you to handle peripheral device issues with confidence. As we move forward, we'll explore even more ways to optimize your Windows 11 experience, ensuring that your digital life remains seamless and enjoyable.

QUIZ: CHAPTER 8 - CONNECTING AND USING PERIPHERAL DEVICES

1. **Which of the following is the first step to set up a wired printer on Windows 11?**

   a. Turn on the printer and connect it to the same Wi-Fi network as your computer.
   b. Plug the printer into a USB port on your computer.
   c. Download and install a third-party printer management tool.
   d. Add the printer using the "Add a printer or scanner" option under Bluetooth & devices.

2. **What is the recommended way to safely eject a USB device from a Windows 11 computer?**

   a. Simply unplug the device without any preparation.
   b. Turn off your computer before unplugging the USB device.
   c. Use the "Safely Remove Hardware and Eject Media" icon on the taskbar.
   d. Run a full scan of the device in Windows Security before unplugging.

3. **When pairing a Bluetooth device, what step is typically required first?**

a. Manually install drivers from the manufacturer's website.
b. Restart your computer to clear existing Bluetooth connections.
c. Put the Bluetooth device into pairing mode.
d. Remove all other connected Bluetooth devices.

4. **Which of the following is a common cause of peripheral devices not being recognized?**

a. Using a USB-C cable instead of a USB-A cable.
b. The computer's display resolution is set too high.
c. Outdated or missing device drivers.
d. The device is placed too close to the monitor.

5. **Why is it important to organize files into folders on an external drive?**

a. To ensure the device does not overheat.
b. To make it easier to find specific files later.
c. To improve the transfer speed of large files.
d. To increase the drive's storage capacity.

9

ADVANCED CUSTOMIZATION AND TIPS

Imagine you're in your favorite room at home, where everything is arranged just the way you like it. The lamp is in the perfect spot for reading, your favorite chair is placed for the best view of the garden, and the remote control is always within reach. Customizing Windows 11 can feel the same way—personalizing the setup to fit your needs and preferences can make your computing experience smoother and more enjoyable. This chapter will explore how to tailor your keyboard shortcuts and hotkeys to save time and reduce the need to reach for your mouse constantly.

9.1 CUSTOMIZING KEYBOARD SHORTCUTS AND HOTKEYS

One of the most significant advantages of customizing keyboard shortcuts is the efficiency they bring to your daily tasks. Imagine being able to open your favorite applications, navigate between different windows, and control media playback without lifting your hands from the keyboard. This saves time and streamlines your workflow, making it easier to accomplish repetitive tasks quickly. For example, if you frequently switch between a web browser and a word processor, setting up a custom shortcut can reduce the time spent moving your mouse and clicking through menus.

To begin customizing your keyboard shortcuts, start by accessing the settings menu. Click on the Start menu and select "Settings," then navigate to "Devices" and click on "Keyboard." Here, you can adjust basic keyboard settings. For more advanced customization, consider using third-party software like AutoHotkey. AutoHotkey allows you to create scripts that automate almost any task, including remapping keys and creating complex shortcuts. To get started with AutoHotkey, download and install the software from its official website. Once installed, you can create a new script by right-clicking on the desktop, selecting "New," and then "AutoHotkey Script." In the script, you can define new shortcuts by specifying the keys you want to remap and the actions they should perform. This flexibility lets you tailor your keyboard setup precisely to your needs.

For those who prefer a simpler approach, Windows 11 offers built-in options for creating custom shortcuts. Open the Settings app, go to "Devices," and then "Keyboard." Here, you can add new shortcuts by clicking on "Add a keyboard shortcut." Enter the key combination you want to use and the action it should perform. For example, you might set Ctrl + Alt + W to open your web browser or Ctrl + Shift + N to create a new document in your word processor. Experiment with different combinations to find the ones that feel most intuitive to you.

Some common custom shortcuts can greatly enhance your productivity. For instance, setting up a shortcut to open frequently used applications can save several seconds each time you need to access them. You might assign Ctrl + Alt + E to open File Explorer or Ctrl + Shift + M to launch your email client. Navigating between virtual desktops is another area where custom shortcuts shine. You can set shortcuts like Ctrl + Alt + Left Arrow and Ctrl + Alt + Right Arrow to switch between desktops seamlessly. Controlling media playback is also easier with custom shortcuts. Assigning keys like Ctrl + Alt + P for play/pause or Ctrl + Alt + Up Arrow for volume up can make managing your media more efficient.

Managing and modifying your custom keyboard shortcuts is just as important as creating them. Over time, you might find that some shortcuts are more useful than others or that your needs change. To edit or delete existing shortcuts, return to the Keyboard settings menu. Here, you'll find a list of all the custom shortcuts you've created. Click on the shortcut you want to modify, then update the key combination or action as needed. If you no longer need a shortcut, simply select it and click "Remove." Keeping your shortcuts organized and relevant ensures that your system remains efficient and easy to use.

By taking the time to customize your keyboard shortcuts and hotkeys, you can transform your Windows 11 experience into a more efficient and enjoyable one, much like arranging your favorite room at home. The benefits of saving time on repetitive tasks and reducing the need for mouse navigation are clear, making this a valuable skill to master.

9.2 MANAGING NOTIFICATIONS AND FOCUS ASSIST

Imagine you're reading a good book, deeply immersed in the story, when suddenly the phone rings, the doorbell chimes, and the dog starts barking. Distractions like these can pull you away from your focus, making it hard to get back into the flow. The same thing happens when you're working on your computer. Constant notifications can interrupt your concentration and slow you down. Managing these notifications effectively can help you stay focused and prioritize what's important.

Let's start by configuring your notification settings. Open the Settings menu by clicking on the Start button and selecting "Settings." From there, navigate to "System" and then "Notifications & actions." This section lets you control which apps can send you notifications and how these notifications appear. You might want to turn off notifications for apps that are less important to you, like games or social media, while keeping them on for essential apps like email or calendar alerts. To do this, scroll down to the list of apps and toggle the switch next to each app to turn notifications on or off. This customization ensures that only the most critical alerts get your attention, reducing unnecessary interruptions and helping you maintain your focus.

Imagine you're working on a project and need to concentrate without being disturbed by incoming notifications. This is where Focus Assist comes in handy. Focus Assist is a feature in Windows 11 that helps you control when and how notifications appear on your screen. To enable Focus Assist, go back to the "System" section in Settings and select "Focus Assist." Here, you can choose from several options based on your needs. You might want to enable Focus Assist during work hours, while gaming, or when giving a presentation. You can set specific rules for each scenario, allowing only priority notifications to come through. For example, during work hours, you might allow notifications from emails and calendar events but block alerts from social media and news apps. This targeted approach helps you stay focused on your tasks without being completely cut off from important updates.

Accessing and clearing notifications is straightforward with the Action Center. To open the Action Center, click on the notification icon located at the far right of the taskbar. It looks like a little bell. This will bring up a panel displaying all recent notifications, organized by app. You can quickly scan through these alerts to see what needs your attention. If you come across a notification you don't need, simply click the "X" next to it to dismiss it. If you want to clear all notifications at once, click on "Clear all" at the top of the Action Center. This feature helps you keep your notification area tidy and ensures that you don't miss any critical alerts amidst the clutter.

When you need to view notifications that you might have missed, the Action Center is your go-to spot. It's like a digital inbox for all your system alerts, emails, calendar reminders, and more. This centralized location makes it easy to manage and review notifications without jumping between different apps. If you ever feel overwhelmed by the number of notifications, take a moment to adjust your settings. Reducing the number of alerts can significantly improve your focus and productivity.

By effectively managing your notifications and using Focus Assist, you can create a more serene and productive computing environment. These tools help you avoid unnecessary interruptions, prioritize essential alerts, and maintain your concentration on the tasks that matter most. This way, you can enjoy your digital activities without constantly being pulled away by distractions.

9.3 SETTING UP VIRTUAL DESKTOPS FOR BETTER ORGANIZATION

Picture your workspace at home. You might have a desk for bills, another for hobbies, and yet another for writing letters. Virtual desktops in Windows 11 serve a similar purpose, helping you organize different tasks and projects efficiently. They allow you to separate work from personal tasks, making your digital workspace less cluttered and more manageable. Whether you're juggling multiple projects or simply want to keep your entertainment apps away from work-related ones, virtual desktops can make your digital life more orderly.

Setting up virtual desktops is straightforward. Start by pressing the Windows key + Tab to open the Task View. Here, you'll see thumbnails of all your open windows. At the top, there's an option to add a new desktop. Click on "New Desktop" to create one. You'll now have two desktops: one for work and one for personal tasks, for example. Switch between them easily by clicking on their thumbnails in Task View or using the shortcut Windows key + Ctrl + Left/Right Arrow. This feature helps you manage your tasks without having all your windows jumbled together.

Organizing your open applications across different virtual desktops is a breeze. In Task View, you can drag and drop windows from one desktop to another. Simply click on the window you want to move and drag it to the desired desktop's thumbnail. Alternatively, right-click on the window, select "Move to," and choose the desktop you want it on. This allows you to keep related apps together, making it easier to switch contexts. For instance, you can have a desktop dedicated to your email and calendar while another desktop holds your web browser and note-taking app for research.

To get the most out of virtual desktops, consider naming them for easy identification. While Windows 11 doesn't offer a built-in feature for naming desktops, you can keep track mentally or use a sticky note on your actual desk as a reminder. Assign specific desktops for different types of tasks. For example, have one for work, another for leisure, and a third for personal projects. This separation helps you stay focused and reduces the temptation to multitask inefficiently. Also, don't hesitate to close unused virtual desktops to free up system resources. If you find yourself not using a particular desktop, hover over its thumbnail in Task View and click the "X" to close it. The open windows will automatically move to the next available desktop, ensuring nothing gets lost.

Using virtual desktops can significantly enhance your productivity by providing a structured environment for your tasks. This feature is especially useful if you're working on multiple projects simultaneously. It helps you keep everything organized and accessible, making it simpler to switch between different activities without losing track of your progress. Whether you're working on a work report, planning a family event, or simply browsing the web, virtual desktops can keep your digital life sorted and stress-free.

9.4 USING WIDGETS FOR QUICK INFORMATION ACCESS

Imagine having a personalized dashboard right on your desktop, giving you real-time updates on the weather, news, calendar events, and more. Windows 11 widgets offer this kind of convenience, making it easy to stay informed without needing to open multiple apps or web pages. These small applications provide dynamic content and can be customized to suit your interests and needs. Whether you want to keep an eye on stock prices, track your daily tasks, or check the weather forecast, widgets can keep you updated at a glance.

To start using widgets, look for the widget icon on the left side of the taskbar, which resembles a small square divided into four smaller squares. Below is an example.

Clicking this icon will open the widget panel, revealing a curated selection of widgets containing various types of information. You can also access the widget panel by pressing the Windows key + W.

Once the panel is open, you'll see default widgets like weather, news, and calendar. These provide basic information, but you can customize and expand this selection to better suit your needs.

Customizing your widget panel is straightforward. To add new widgets, click the plus sign (+) at the top right of the panel. This opens a gallery of available widgets, where you can browse and choose the ones that interest you. Simply click "Add" next to the widget you want, and it will appear on your panel. If you want to remove a widget, click the three-dot menu in the upper-right corner of the widget and select "Remove." Rearranging widgets is as easy as clicking and dragging them to your preferred position on the panel. This way, you can organize your dashboard to high-light the most important information at a glance.

Customizing the content within each widget ensures you get the most relevant updates. For instance, the news widget can be tailored to show topics that interest you. Click the three-dot menu on the news widget and select "Customize." Here, you can choose categories like technology, sports, or entertainment. Similarly, the weather widget can be adjusted to display the forecast for your specific location. Click on the weather widget, choose "Settings," and enter your city or postal code. The calendar widget can sync with your Microsoft account, showing your events and reminders. Simply link your account and select which calendars you want to display.

To optimize your widget usage, regularly update your preferences to reflect any changes in your interests. If you start following a new hobby, add relevant widgets to keep up with the latest updates and trends. Widgets can complement your daily routines by providing timely reminders and information. For example, a stock ticker widget can keep you informed about market fluctuations if you're an investor. A to-do list widget can help you manage daily tasks, ensuring you stay on track throughout the day. Keeping the widget panel organized and free from clutter enhances its usability. Remove any widgets you no longer find useful and rearrange the remaining ones to keep your dashboard clean and efficient.

Widgets in Windows 11 are a powerful tool for staying informed and organized. They bring real-time updates and essential information directly to your desktop, saving you the hassle of opening multiple apps or web pages. By customizing and organizing your widgets, you can create a personalized dashboard that keeps you connected to the information that matters most to you, all within a few clicks.

9.5 PRACTICAL TIPS AND SHORTCUTS FOR EVERYDAY TASKS

Imagine having a toolbox that allows you to complete tasks faster and with less effort. That's what practical tips and shortcuts in Windows 11 offer. Knowing a few key shortcuts can make your computing experience smoother and more efficient. For instance, pressing the Windows key + D instantly shows your desktop, minimizing all open windows. This is handy when you need to access files or shortcuts on your desktop quickly. Another useful shortcut is Windows key + L, which locks your computer. This is particularly useful if you need to step away from your desk but want to ensure your computer remains secure. Additionally, pressing Ctrl + Shift + Esc opens the Task Manager directly, allowing you to quickly manage running applications and processes without navigating through multiple menus.

Snap Layouts are another feature that can greatly enhance your productivity. They allow you to organize and manage open windows quickly and easily. To use Snap Layouts, hover your mouse over the maximize button in the upper-right corner of any window. A grid of layout options will appear, showing different ways to arrange your windows. Click on the desired layout, and your window will snap into place. You can then select other windows to fill the remaining slots in the layout. This feature is particularly useful when working on multiple documents or applications simultaneously, as it keeps everything organized and within easy reach.

Clipboard history is a feature that can make managing copied items much simpler. To enable clipboard history, go to Settings, then System, and click on Clipboard. Toggle the switch to turn on clipboard history. Once enabled, you can access it by pressing the Windows key + V. This brings up a list of items you've copied recently, allowing you to paste any of them with a click. This is especially useful when working with multiple pieces of text or images, as it saves you from having to copy and paste items one at a time. You can also pin frequently used items to the clipboard history for even quicker access.

Efficient file management is crucial for keeping your digital workspace tidy and easy to navigate. One practical tip is to use Quick Access in File Explorer. Quick Access is a section in the navigation pane that shows your frequently used folders and recent files. You can pin your most-used folders to Quick Access by right-clicking on them and selecting "Pin to Quick Access." This makes it easy to access important files and folders without digging through multiple directories. Another tip is to create shortcuts for frequently used folders. Right-click on a folder, select "Create shortcut," and place the shortcut on your desktop or in a convenient location. This saves time when you need to access these folders quickly.

Organizing files with descriptive names and consistent naming conventions can also improve file management. Instead of using vague names like "Document1" or "IMG_1234," use descriptive names that indicate the content or purpose of the file, such as "Tax_Return_2023" or "Family_Vacation_Photo." Consistent naming conventions make it easier to locate files and keep your folders organized. For example, you might use a format like "YYYY_MM_DD_Description" for naming files, ensuring they are sorted chronologically and easy to identify.

By incorporating these practical tips and shortcuts into your daily routine, you can streamline your workflow and make your Windows 11 experience more efficient and enjoyable. Whether you're managing multiple applications, organizing your files, or simply navigating your desktop, these tools and techniques provide a foundation for a smoother, more productive computing experience.

WRAPPING UP CHAPTER 9

In this chapter, we've explored advanced customization options and practical tips that can make your Windows 11 experience more efficient and tailored to your needs. From creating custom keyboard shortcuts and managing notifications to setting up virtual desktops and using widgets, these tools help you organize your digital workspace and streamline everyday tasks.

QUIZ: CHAPTER 9 - ADVANCED CUSTOMIZATION AND TIPS

1. **What is a key benefit of customizing keyboard shortcuts in Windows 11?**

   a. It increases your computer's processing speed.
   b. It makes repetitive tasks faster and reduces the need for a mouse.
   c. It disables unnecessary system features.
   d. It automatically creates backup files for documents.

2. **What is Focus Assist designed to help you do?**

   a. Increase the brightness of your screen.
   b. Block all notifications from appearing.
   c. Control when and how notifications appear so you can stay focused.
   d. Automatically close unused applications.

3. **How can you create a new virtual desktop in Windows 11?**

   a. Press Windows key + Tab and click "New Desktop."
   b. Right-click the desktop and select "Add Virtual Desktop."
   c. Open File Explorer and choose "Create Virtual Desktop."
   d. Use Windows key + Alt + D.

4. **Which keyboard shortcut opens clipboard history in Windows 11?**

a. Ctrl + V
b. Windows key + V
c. Ctrl + Alt + C
d. Windows key + C

5. **What is a suggested naming convention to keep your files organized?**

a. Use a random assortment of numbers and letters.
b. Rely on automatically generated file names.
c. Use descriptive names and a consistent format like "YYYY_MM_DD_Description."
d. Keep file names as short as possible without descriptions.

10

TROUBLESHOOTING COMMON ISSUES

You're working on an important document or enjoying a video call with your grandchildren, and suddenly, your application crashes. It's a frustrating experience, especially when you're unsure why it happened. Understanding how to troubleshoot software crashes can save you time and reduce stress. This chapter will guide you through identifying the cause of these crashes, updating or reinstalling problematic software, and using Windows Troubleshooters to diagnose and fix issues.

10.1 TROUBLESHOOTING SOFTWARE CRASHES

When an application crashes, the first step is to determine why it's happening. Often, the software will display an error message or code that can provide clues. These messages might seem cryptic, but they're valuable for diagnosing the problem. Start by noting down any error codes or messages that appear. For instance, you might see a message like "Application Error: 0xc0000005." This might not mean much at first glance, but it's a key piece of information.

To dig deeper, you can use the Event Viewer, a built-in tool in Windows 11 that logs various system events, including application crashes. To access the Event Viewer, press the Windows key + R, type "eventvwr.msc," and press Enter. Once the Event Viewer opens, navigate to the 'Windows Logs' section and select 'Application.' Here, you'll find a list of application-related events. Look for entries marked with a red error icon. Clicking on these entries will provide more details about the crash, including the error code and any related files. The Event Viewer can be over-whelming at first, but focusing on the red error entries helps narrow down the search.

Another useful tool is the Reliability Monitor, which provides a timeline of your system's reliability history. To access it, type "Control Panel" into the search bar, open it, and navigate to System and Security > Security and Maintenance > View reliability history. The Reliability Monitor categorizes issues into application failures, Windows failures, miscellaneous failures, warnings, and informational messages. This timeline helps you pinpoint when the crashes started and what changes might have triggered them, such as recent software updates or new installations.

Once you've identified the potential cause of the crash, the next step is to update or reinstall the problematic software. Many applications have built-in update features that automatically check for the latest versions. Open the application and navigate to its settings or help menu to find the update option. If an update is available, follow the prompts to install it. Updating often resolves compatibility issues and bugs that cause crashes.

If updating doesn't solve the problem, consider reinstalling the software. First, uninstall the application by going to Settings > Apps > Apps & features. Find the application in the list, click on it, and select "Uninstall." Once it's uninstalled, visit the official website of the software to download the latest version. Follow the installation instructions provided on the website. Ensure that the software is compatible with Windows 11 to avoid future issues. Compatibility information is usually available on the software's download page.

Windows 11 also provides built-in troubleshooters to help diagnose and fix software issues. To access these troubleshooters, go to Settings > Update & Security > Troubleshoot. Here, you'll find a list of troubleshooters categorized by different issues. For software crashes, the "Program Compatibility Troubleshooter" and "Windows Store Apps" troubleshooter are particularly useful. Select the appropriate troubleshooter, follow the on-screen instructions, and let Windows diagnose the problem. These troubleshooters can automatically fix common issues or provide recommendations for manual fixes.

Maintaining a stable software environment is crucial for preventing future crashes. One of the best practices is to keep all your software updated. Developers regularly release updates to fix bugs and improve compatibility with the latest operating systems. Enable automatic updates whenever possible, both for Windows and individual applications. This ensures you always have the latest fixes and features.

Another important tip is to avoid running unnecessary background applications. Too many applications running simultaneously can strain your system's resources, leading to crashes. Use the Task Manager (Ctrl + Shift + Es to monitor and manage running applications. Close any that you don't need to free up system resources. This practice not only prevents crashes but also improves overall system performance.

Regularly cleaning up temporary files and caches can also help maintain stability. Over time, these files accumulate and can cause performance issues. Use the built-in Disk Cleanup tool to remove unnecessary files. Type "Disk Cleanup" in the search bar, select the drive you want to clean (usually C:), and follow the prompts. This simple maintenance task can free up space and reduce the likelihood of crashes.

Ensuring your system has adequate resources, such as RAM and storage, is another key factor. Insufficient RAM can cause applications to crash, especially if you're running multiple programs simultaneously. If you frequently experience crashes, consider upgrading your RAM. Similarly, ensure you have enough free storage space on your hard drive. A nearly full hard drive can slow down your system and trigger crashes. Regularly check your storage usage and delete or move files to free up space.

In conclusion, troubleshooting software crashes involves identifying the cause, updating or reinstalling software, and using Windows troubleshooters. By keeping your software updated, managing background applications, cleaning up temporary files, and ensuring adequate system resources, you can maintain a stable and efficient computing environment. These proactive steps not only prevent crashes but also enhance your overall experience with Windows 11.

10.2 FIXING INTERNET CONNECTIVITY ISSUES

There you are, ready to check your emails or watch a favorite show, but your internet connection isn't cooperating. Diagnosing connectivity problems can seem daunting, but with some straightforward steps, you can often resolve the issue quickly. Start by checking the network status on your computer. Go to Settings > Network & Internet. Here, you'll see an overview of your network connections. If there's an issue, Windows will often display a message or a yellow warning icon. This initial check can give you a quick indication of what might be wrong.

Next, use the Network Troubleshooter built into Windows 11. This tool can automatically detect and fix common network problems. To access it, go back to Settings > Network & Internet > Status, and then click on the Network Troubleshooter link. Follow the on-screen instructions. The troubleshooter will check various network settings and attempt to resolve any issues it finds. It's a simple yet powerful tool that can save you a lot of hassle.

Sometimes, the issue might be with the physical connections. Ensure that all cables are securely plugged in. Check the Ethernet cable if you're using a wired connection. Make sure it's firmly connected to both your computer and the router. For Wi-Fi users, verify that the router is powered on and working correctly. You can do this by looking at the indicator lights on the router. If the lights are off or flashing unusually, there might be a problem with the router itself. Restarting your router can often fix minor glitches. Unplug the router, wait for about 30 seconds, and then plug it back in. Give it a couple of minutes to reboot fully.

If these steps don't resolve the issue, you might need to reset your network settings. Resetting the network settings restores all network-related configurations to their default state, which can resolve persistent connectivity problems. To reset your network settings, go to Settings > Network & Internet > Status. Scroll down and click on Network reset. A prompt will appear, explaining what will happen. Confirm the action by clicking Reset now. Your computer will restart, and all network adapters will be reset to their factory settings. After the reboot, reconnect to your Wi-Fi network by entering the password.

Sometimes, outdated or corrupted network drivers can cause connectivity issues. Updating these drivers can improve performance and compatibility. To update your network drivers, first, open the Device Manager by typing "Device Manager" into the search bar and selecting it from the results. In Device Manager, expand the Network adapters section. You'll see a list of network devices. Right-click on your network adapter (it might be labeled as Wireless Network Adapter for Wi-Fi or Ethernet Adapter for wired connections) and select Update driver. Choose the option to search automatically for updated driver software. Windows will search online for the latest drivers and install them if available. If the automatic search doesn't find anything, visit the manufacturer's website to download the latest driver.

Optimizing Wi-Fi performance can also make a significant difference in your connectivity experience. Start by positioning your router in a central location within your home. This helps ensure that the Wi-Fi signal reaches all areas effectively. Avoid placing the router near walls, large metal objects, or other electronic devices that could cause interference. Elevating the router can also improve signal strength. If you live in a larger home or one with thick walls, consider using Wi-Fi extenders or a mesh network system. Wi-Fi extenders boost the signal to reach further areas, while mesh systems use multiple devices to create a seamless network throughout your home.

Changing the Wi-Fi channel can help avoid interference from other nearby networks. Most routers are set to auto-select the best channel, but sometimes manually selecting a less crowded channel can improve performance. Access your router's settings by typing its IP address into a web browser (common addresses are 192.168.1.1 or 192.168.0.1). Log in with the router's username and password (usually found on a sticker on the router). Navigate to the wireless settings section and try changing the channel to one that isn't being heavily used by other networks in your area.

Ensuring your router's firmware is up to date is another crucial step. Firmware updates often include performance improvements and security patches. To update your router's firmware, access the router's settings as described earlier. Look for a section labeled Firmware Update or Router Update. Follow the instructions to check for and install any available updates. This process might take a few minutes, and the router will likely reboot once the update is complete.

By following these steps, you can diagnose and resolve many common internet connectivity issues. Checking the network status, using the Network Troubleshooter, and verifying physical connections are good starting points. Resetting network settings and updating network drivers can address more persistent problems. Optimizing Wi-Fi performance through proper router placement, using extenders, changing channels, and updating firmware ensures a stable and fast connection. These measures help maintain a reliable internet connection, allowing you to stay connected and enjoy your online activities without interruptions.

10.3 RESOLVING COMMON PRINTER PROBLEMS

Imagine you're about to print an important document, and suddenly, your printer refuses to cooperate. Printer issues can be incredibly frustrating, but many common problems are easy to diagnose and fix. The first step in addressing printer issues is to check the printer's status and any error messages that may appear on the device or your computer. These messages often provide clues about what's wrong. For instance, an error message might indicate a paper jam, low ink, or connectivity issues. Make sure to address these specific errors as they arise.

Next, ensure that your printer is properly connected to your computer. If you're using a USB connection, check that the cable is securely plugged into both the printer and your computer. For Wi-Fi printers, verify that the printer is connected to the same network as your computer. You can usually find the network settings on the printer's control panel. If the printer isn't showing up on your network, you might need to reconnect it through the Wi-Fi setup process. Additionally, make sure the printer is turned on and has paper loaded in the tray.

Once you've confirmed that the printer is physically connected and powered on, verify its availability in Devices and Printers. To do this, open the Control Panel and navigate to Devices and Printers. Here, you should see an icon representing your printer. If the printer isn't listed, it means your computer isn't recognizing the device. In this case, try unplugging the printer and plugging it back in. You can also click "Add a printer" to manually search for and add the device. This step ensures that your computer acknowledges the printer and is ready to send print jobs to it.

Updating printer drivers can resolve many issues, especially if your printer isn't functioning correctly after a Windows update. To update your printer drivers, open Device Manager by typing "Device Manager" in the search bar and selecting it from the results. Once in Device Manager, expand the Printers section, right-click on your printer, and select "Update driver." Choose the option to search automatically for updated driver software. Windows will search for and install any available updates. If no updates are found, visit the printer manufacturer's website to download the latest driver. Follow the installation instructions provided on the website to ensure the driver is installed correctly. If updating doesn't help, you might need to uninstall and reinstall the driver. Right-click on the printer in Device Manager, select "Uninstall device," and then reinstall the driver from the manufacturer's website.

Print jobs can sometimes get stuck in the print queue, preventing new jobs from being processed. To clear the print queue, open Devices and Printers, right-click on your printer, and select "See what's printing." This opens the print queue window, where you can see all pending print jobs. Right-click on each job and select "Cancel" to clear the queue. Once all jobs are canceled, try printing your document again. Clearing the print queue often resolves issues where documents aren't printing despite the printer being ready and connected.

Maintaining your printer in good working condition is essential for preventing future issues. Regularly clean the printer, including the printheads and rollers, to ensure smooth operation. Most printers have a maintenance menu accessible through the control panel or printer software on your computer. Use the built-in tools for printhead alignment and cleaning cycles to keep the printer in optimal condition. Keeping ink or toner levels adequate is also crucial. Low ink or toner can result in poor print quality and can sometimes cause the printer to refuse to print. Regularly check the ink or toner levels and replace cartridges as needed.

Updating the printer's firmware can provide performance improvements and fix bugs that might be causing issues. To update the firmware, visit the printer manufacturer's website and download the latest firmware update for your model. Follow the instructions provided to install the update. This process might involve connecting the printer to your computer via USB or using a memory card. Firmware updates can resolve many issues and ensure your printer operates with the latest features and improvements.

By following these steps, you can diagnose and resolve common printer problems, ensuring your device remains reliable and efficient. Checking the printer's status and connectivity, updating drivers, clearing print queues, and performing regular mainte-nance are all key practices. These proactive measures help prevent issues and keep your printer in top condition, allowing you to print documents smoothly whenever needed.

Maintaining a well-functioning printer not only makes everyday tasks easier but also ensures you're prepared for important moments, like printing boarding passes, tickets, or cherished family photos. Understanding how to troubleshoot and maintain your printer enhances your overall experience with Windows 11, making your digital interactions more seamless and enjoyable.

QUIZ: CHAPTER 10 - TROUBLESHOOTING COMMON ISSUES

Questions:

1. **Which Windows tool provides a timeline of reliability history to help identify when application crashes started?**

   a. Task Manager
   b. Reliability Monitor
   c. Event Viewer
   d. Disk Cleanup

2. **What is one of the first steps you should take when an application crashes?**

   a. Immediately reinstall the operating system.
   b. Search for the application's icon in the taskbar.
   c. Note down any error messages or codes that appear.
   d. Close all other running applications.

3. **If your internet connection isn't working, which built-in Windows tool can you use to automatically detect and fix common network problems?**

a. Network Troubleshooter
b. Device Manager
c. Task Manager
d. Disk Cleanup

4. **What action can help improve Wi-Fi performance if the signal is weak in certain areas of your home?**

a. Changing the background color of your desktop.
b. Using Wi-Fi extenders or a mesh network system.
c. Adding more Ethernet cables.
d. Turning off automatic updates.

5. **What is one way to clear stuck print jobs that prevent other documents from printing?**

a. Open Task Manager and end the "Explorer.exe" process.
b. Remove and reinstall the printer drivers.
c. Access the printer queue and cancel all pending print jobs.
d. Unplug the printer and leave it disconnected for 24 hours.

CONCLUSION

We've journeyed together through the various facets of Windows 11, exploring its features and functionalities step-by-step. From the initial setup and personalization to mastering file management and enhancing security, you have absorbed a wealth of knowledge designed to make your digital experience seamless and enjoyable.

We began by getting acquainted with the basics of Windows 11, guiding you through unboxing your new device, completing the initial setup, and understanding the desktop layout. These foundational steps built your confidence in navigating your new system. By learning how to connect to the internet and browse safely, you gained the ability to explore the web with ease and security.

Personalization allowed you to make Windows 11 truly your own. You discovered how changing backgrounds, themes, and taskbar settings can transform your workspace into a reflection of your style. Adjusting display settings and setting up user accounts ensured that your computer catered to your specific needs.

Installing and managing software opened up a world of possibilities, from finding useful apps in the Microsoft Store to safely downloading software from the internet. You learned how to keep your system clutter-free by managing updates, uninstalling unnecessary applications, and utilizing built-in Windows apps effectively.

Mastering file management was like becoming the librarian of your digital world. Navigating File Explorer, creating and organizing folders, and using external storage devices equipped you to keep your files tidy and accessible. Regular backups became a safety net, protecting your important data from unexpected loss.

Staying connected through email and social media expanded your communication horizons. Setting up email accounts, managing contacts, and using video call applications ensured you stayed in touch with loved ones. Exploring social media platforms allowed you to share moments and engage with friends and family in new ways.

Enhancing security and privacy was paramount to safeguarding your digital life. Setting up Windows Defender, configuring privacy settings, and recognizing online scams fortified your defenses. Managing passwords and using two-factor authentication added an extra layer of security, keeping your personal information safe.

Connecting and using peripheral devices, such as printers, scanners, and Bluetooth gadgets, broadened your computer's capabilities. Troubleshooting common issues ensured that these devices worked smoothly, enhancing your overall experience.

Advanced customization and practical tips rounded out your journey, making Windows 11 work for you. Customizing keyboard shortcuts, managing notifications, and setting up virtual desktops streamlined your workflow. Using widgets for quick information access and applying everyday tips made your digital interactions more efficient.

The key takeaways from this book should empower you to use Windows 11 with confidence. You've learned how to personalize your setup, manage files effectively, stay connected with loved ones, and keep your system secure. These skills are not just technical; they are gateways to a more enriching digital life.

Remember, the aim of this book was to build your confidence and independence. You have the knowledge and tools to navigate Windows 11 effortlessly. Don't be afraid to explore and experiment. Mistakes are part of the learning process, and you now have the skills to troubleshoot and resolve issues as they arise.

Now, it's time to take action. Apply what you've learned. Change that desktop background to a photo you love. Set up a video call with your grandkids. Organize your files into neatly labeled folders. Enable two-factor authentication on your email account. Each small step you take reinforces your learning and builds your confidence.

As you continue to explore and use Windows 11, remember that you're not alone. My passion for helping seniors and beginners overcome tech challenges drives every page of this book. I am here to support you on this journey. Technology can be daunting, but with patience and practice, you will find it becomes a valuable ally in your daily life.

Thank you for allowing me to guide you through this digital adventure. Your willingness to learn and embrace new skills is truly inspiring. Keep exploring, keep learning, and most importantly, enjoy the journey. Your digital world is now at your fingertips, and I am confident you will navigate it with ease and joy.

QUIZ ANSWERS

1. **What should you do first when unboxing your new Windows 11 device?**

   Answer: Handle items carefully and check for all necessary components

2. **Why is it recommended to use a surge protector when setting up your new device?**

   Answer: To protect your device from electrical surges

3. **What is the purpose of selecting your language and region during the initial setup?**

   Answer: To set default system preferences, such as language and time zone

4. **Which of the following is NOT part of the Windows 11 desktop layout?**

   Answer: File Explorer menu bar

5. **What is the function of the Alt + Tab keyboard shortcut in Windows 11?**

   Answer: To switch between open applications

ANSWERS: CHAPTER 2 - CONNECTING TO THE INTERNET

1. **What is one primary advantage of using Ethernet over Wi-Fi?**

   Answer: It provides a stable and faster connection.

2. **Where can you find your Wi-Fi password if you don't remember it?**

   Answer: Printed on your router or provided by your internet service provider.

3. **What feature of Microsoft Edge protects you from phishing and malware?**

   Answer: SmartScreen filter.

4. **How can you save a website to access it later in Microsoft Edge?**

   Answer: Click the star icon in the address bar to add it to bookmarks or favorites.

5. **What is a key characteristic of a strong password?**

   Answer: It includes a mix of letters, numbers, and special characters.

ANSWERS: CHAPTER 3 - PERSONALIZING YOUR WINDOWS 11 EXPERIENCE

1. **How can you set a slideshow as your desktop background in Windows 11?**

   Answer: Go to Settings > Personalization > Background, select "Slideshow," and choose a folder of images.

2. **What is the purpose of pinning apps to the taskbar?**

   Answer: To make apps accessible with a single click.

3. **Which feature in Windows 11 helps reduce eye strain during late-night use?**

   Answer: Night light.

4. **What is a Microsoft account's main advantage compared to a local account?**

   Answer: It syncs settings and files across multiple devices.

5. **Which accessibility feature reads aloud the text and buttons on your screen?**

   Answer: Narrator.

1. **What is the easiest way to find and install apps on Windows 11?**

   Answer: Browsing and installing apps from the Microsoft Store.

2. **What is a recommended way to avoid installing unwanted programs or toolbars during software installation?**

   Answer: Carefully review each installation step and uncheck unnecessary options.

3. **Where can you find the option to uninstall applications in Windows 11?**

   Answer: Under Settings > Apps > Apps & features.

4. **How can you change which program opens a specific file type by default?**

   Answer: Go to Settings > Apps > Default apps and choose by file type.

5. **Which built-in app can help you manage multiple email accounts in one place?**

   Answer: Mail

ANSWERS: CHAPTER 5 - MASTERING FILE MANAGEMENT

1. **What is the keyboard shortcut to open File Explorer?**

   Answer: Windows key + E

2. **Which view in File Explorer provides additional details about each file, such as size and date modified?**

   Answer: Details view

3. **What is the difference between copying and moving a file?**

   Answer: Copying creates a duplicate, while moving changes the file's location without creating a duplicate.

4. **What is the purpose of the Recycle Bin?**

   Answer: To store deleted files temporarily so they can be recovered if needed.

5. **What is the primary function of File History in Windows 11?**

   Answer: To create automatic backups of important files.

1. **What is a popular feature of Gmail that makes it a strong choice for many users?**

   Answer: Integration with Google services like Google Drive and Google Docs

2. **Which folder in Gmail contains messages that you started but haven't sent yet?**

   Answer: Drafts

3. **What is the purpose of organizing contacts into groups in an email address book?**

   Answer: To categorize contacts for easier email communication

4. **What is one of the main advantages of using social media platforms like Facebook or Instagram?**

   Answer: They allow you to quickly connect and share updates with friends and family.

5. **What is a helpful practice when receiving emails with attachments?**

   Answer: Verify the sender's identity before downloading the attachment.**Answers:**

ANSWERS: CHAPTER 7 -ENHANCING SECURITY AND PRIVACY

1. **What is one of the primary benefits of Windows Defender's real-time protection?**

   Answer: It monitors your system continuously and neutralizes threats immediately.

2. **Which setting can be adjusted to limit apps' access to your location, camera, and microphone?**

   Answer: Privacy & Security > App permissions

3. **What is the best practice when receiving an email that appears to be from a known organization but asks for sensitive information?**

   Answer: Verify the email's legitimacy by contacting the organization through known contact details.

4. **What is the purpose of using two-factor authentication (2F?**

   Answer: To add an extra layer of security by requiring a second form of verification.

5. **What should you look for to ensure a website is secure for online shopping?**

   Answer: HTTPS in the URL and a padlock icon.

ANSWERS: CHAPTER 8 - CONNECTING AND USING PERIPHERAL DEVICES

1. **Which of the following is the first step to set up a wired printer on Windows 11?**

   Answer: Plug the printer into a USB port on your computer.

2. **What is the recommended way to safely eject a USB device from a Windows 11 computer?**

   Answer: Use the "Safely Remove Hardware and Eject Media" icon on the taskbar.

3. **When pairing a Bluetooth device, what step is typically required first?**

   Answer: Put the Bluetooth device into pairing mode.

4. **Which of the following is a common cause of peripheral devices not being recognized?**

   Answer: Outdated or missing device drivers.

5. **Why is it important to organize files into folders on an external drive?**

   Answer: To make it easier to find specific files later.

1. **What is a key benefit of customizing keyboard
   shortcuts in Windows 11?**

   Answer: It makes repetitive tasks faster and reduces the
   need for a mouse.

2. **What is Focus Assist designed to help you do?**

   Answer: Control when and how notifications appear so
   you can stay focused.

3. **How can you create a new virtual desktop in
   Windows 11?**

   Answer: Press Windows key + Tab and click "New
   Desktop."

4. **Which keyboard shortcut opens clipboard history in
   Windows 11?**

   Answer: Windows key + V

5. **What is a suggested naming convention to keep your
   files organized?**

   Answer: Use descriptive names and a consistent format like
   "YYYY_MM_DD_Description."

1. **Which Windows tool provides a timeline of reliability history to help identify when application crashes started?**

   Answer: Reliability Monitor

2. **What is one of the first steps you should take when an application crashes?**

   Answer: Note down any error messages or codes that appear.

3. **If your internet connection isn't working, which built-in Windows tool can you use to automatically detect and fix common network problems?**

   Answer: Network Troubleshooter

4. **What action can help improve Wi-Fi performance if the signal is weak in certain areas of your home?**

   Answer: Using Wi-Fi extenders or a mesh network system.

5. **What is one way to clear stuck print jobs that prevent other documents from printing?**

   Answer: Access the printer queue and cancel all pending print jobs.

REFERENCES

How to set up new laptop running Windows 11 in 2024 https://www.windowscentral.com/software-apps/windows-11/how-to-set-up-new-laptop-running-windows-11-2022

How to customize the Windows 11 Start menu https://www.tomsguide.com/how-to/how-to-customize-the-windows-11-start-menu

Windows keyboard shortcuts - Microsoft Support https://support.microsoft.com/en-us/windows/windows-keyboard-shortcuts-3d444b08-3a00-abd6-67da-ecfc07e86b98

Windows 11 Accessibility Features https://www.microsoft.com/en-us/windows/accessibility-features

Connect to a Wi-Fi network in Windows https://support.microsoft.com/en-us/windows/connect-to-a-wi-fi-network-in-windows-1f881677-b569-0cd5-010d-e3cd3579d263

Get connected when setting up your Windows 11 PC https://support.microsoft.com/en-us/windows/get-connected-when-setting-up-your-windows-11-pc-50dca26f-40d5-4c3b-853c-e972dafb7e08

Microsoft Edge Tutorial for Beginners https://ansonalex.com/tutorials/windows/microsoft-edge-tutorial/

The Senior's Guide to Online Safety https://connectsafely.org/seniors-guide-to-online-safety/

Change your desktop background image https://support.microsoft.com/en-us/windows/change-your-desktop-background-image-175618be-4cf1-c159-2785-ec2238b433a8

How to customize the Windows 11 Start menu https://www.tomsguide.com/how-to/how-to-customize-the-windows-11-start-menu

Make the computer easier to see https://support.microsoft.com/en-us/windows/make-the-computer-easier-to-see-9ac09d27-b913-66dc-2c57-4a804d650d95

Set up your device to work with accessibility in Microsoft 365 https://support.microsoft.com/en-us/office/set-up-your-device-to-work-with-accessibility-in-microsoft-365-a0ca81c1-fa3e-417e-9d3b-78b8816fce58

How to Use the Microsoft Store in Windows 11 https://www.pcmag.com/how-to/how-to-use-the-microsoft-store-in-windows-11

Safely Downloading and Installing Software https://globalgurus.org/safely-downloading-and-installing-software-a-comprehensive-guide/

Best free software uninstaller of 2024 https://www.techradar.com/best/best-free-software-uninstallers

How to get started with the new Outlook app for Windows 11 https://www.windowscentral.com/software-apps/windows-11/how-to-get-started-with-the-new-outlook-app-for-windows-11

The ultimate guide to File Explorer on Windows 11 https://www.xda-developers.com/file-explorer-windows-11/

Organize Your Files in New Folders | Windows Learning ... https://www.microsoft.com/en-us/windows/learning-center/create-new-folders-to-organize-files

Move your files to a new Windows PC using an external ... https://support.microsoft.com/en-us/windows/move-your-files-to-a-new-windows-pc-using-an-external-storage-device-dd139b2e-bc73-4431-8e6e-c96e10dffdf5#:~

How to Set Up and Use File History on Windows 11 https://www.makeuseof.com/windows-11-file-history-guide/

Gmail Account Set up and Management for Seniors https://onesupport.com/gmail-set-up-for-seniors/#:~

Manage contacts in Outlook https://support.microsoft.com/en-us/office/manage-contacts-in-outlook-e5fc2d01-2a15-46fe-90f2-b8ebea8f1b29

How to Send an Email with an Attachment (for Beginners) https://lifehacker.com/how-to-send-an-email-with-an-attachment-for-beginners-5803366

How to Set Up Social Media for Your Business https://www.mintformations.co.uk/how-to-set-up-social-media/

How to get started with Microsoft Defender Antivirus on ... https://www.windowscentral.com/software-apps/windows-11/how-to-get-started-with-microsoft-defender-antivirus-on-windows-11

The Best Antivirus Software for 2024 https://www.pcmag.com/picks/the-best-antivirus-protection

Change privacy settings in Windows https://support.microsoft.com/en-us/windows/change-privacy-settings-in-windows-55466b7b-14de-c230-3ece-6b75557c5227

How to Recognize and Avoid Phishing Scams https://consumer.ftc.gov/articles/how-recognize-and-avoid-phishing-scams

Add a printer or scanner in Windows https://support.microsoft.com/en-us/windows/add-a-printer-or-scanner-in-windows-14d9a442-0bcb-e11c-7a6c-63f00efae79f

Pair a Bluetooth device in Windows - Microsoft Support https://support.microsoft.com/en-us/windows/pair-a-bluetooth-device-in-windows-2be7b51f-6ae9-b757-a3b9-95ee40c3e242#:~

How to manage storage devices on Windows 11 https://www.windowscentral.com/how-manage-storage-devices-windows-11

Why Won't Your PC Recognize Peripheral Devices? 2024 Dr ... https://dr-it.co.uk/why-wont-your-pc-recognize-peripheral-devices/

How to change keyboard shortcuts in Windows 11 https://www.tomsguide.com/how-to/how-to-change-keyboard-shortcuts-in-windows-11

How to use Focus Assist and Notifications settings in ... https://www.techrepublic.com/article/how-to-use-focus-assist-notifications-settings-windows-11-22h2/

How to Use Virtual Desktops on Windows 11 https://www.howtogeek.com/796349/how-to-use-virtual-desktops-on-windows-11/

How to Use Widgets in Windows 11 https://www.lifewire.com/use-widgets-windows-11-6751639

How to View Windows Crash Logs and Error Logs? https://www.stellarinfo.co.in/blog/how-to-view-windows-crash-logs-and-error-logs/

How to Reset Network Settings in Windows 11 https://www.lifewire.com/reset-network-settings-in-windows-11-5194111

How to download and install the latest printer drivers https://support.microsoft.com/en-us/windows/how-to-download-and-install-the-latest-printer-drivers-4ff66446-a2ab-b77f-46f4-a6d3fe4bf661

Windows troubleshooting tips, tools, and techniques https://www.computerworld.com/article/1612986/windows-troubleshooting-tips-tools-techniques.html

www.ingramcontent.com/pod-product-compliance
Lightning Source LLC
LaVergne TN
LVHW051339050326
832903LV00031B/3642